# EVALUATION
# AND EFFECTIVE
# PUBLIC MANAGEMENT

D1170545

1983

LITTLE, BROWN FOUNDATIONS OF PUBLIC MANAGEMENT SERIES

# Evaluation and Effective Public Management

Joseph S. Wholey

University of Southern California
Washington Public Affairs Center

Little, Brown and Company

Boston          Toronto

**Library of Congress Cataloging in Publication Data**

Wholey, Joseph S.
  Evaluation and effective management.

  (Little, Brown foundations of public management
series)
  Bibliography: p.
  Includes indexes.
  1. Public administration — Evaluation. I. Title.
II. Series.
JF1411.W46 1983     350.007'6     82-18647
ISBN 0-316-93782-7
ISBN 0-316-93783-5 (pbk.)

Design by David Ford

Little, Brown Foundations of Public Management Series

Library of Congress Catalog Card No. 82-18647

ISBN 0-316-93782-7
ISBN 0-316-93783-5 {pbk.}

9 8 7 6 5 4 3 2 1

ALP

Published simultaneously in Canada
by Little, Brown & Company (Canada) Limited

Printed in the United States of America

For Skef and Kate

# Contents

## PART I: EFFECTIVE MANAGEMENT

Introduction/ Problems and Solutions/ Examples of
Results-Oriented Management/ Conclusion/ Notes to
Chapter 1

## PART II: GETTING AGREEMENT ON REALISTIC, RESULTS-ORIENTED OBJECTIVES AND PERFORMANCE INDICATORS

Introduction/ Problems Inhibiting Results-Oriented
Management and Useful Program Evaluation/ Origin and
Evolution of Evaluability Assessment/ The Evaluability
Assessment Process/ Conclusion/ Notes to Chapter 2

## PART IV: USING EVALUATION TO STIMULATE
## EFFECTIVE MANAGEMENT

# List of Figures and Tables

**Figures**

# Foreword
to the
Little, Brown
Foundations
of Public
Management
Series

Over the past several years growth in interest and concern about the management of government has paralleled the growth of government itself. As a result, the study of public administration has been infused with new ideas and new approaches, giving it a new intellectual vitality and excitement. This new life has spread to those who must grapple with public problems as well as to those who study, teach, and conduct research about the public sector.

The books in the Little, Brown Foundations of Public Management Series are intended to convey the new dynamism of public management. Each is designed to analyze a major aspect of public management — for example, intergovernment relations, budgeting, human resources, decision making, organization behavior, and program management — by examining closely the blend of administrative, legal, political, and economic factors in producing public services. The authors have approached their task by integrating the latest theoretical thinking with findings from empirical research to account for the behavior of public managers and organizations. Each author has stepped beyond the boundaries of one discipline to search widely for perspectives, approaches, and research that might improve our understanding of public-sector operations and enhance governmental performance.

The theme of improving governmental performance lies at the heart of Joseph S. Wholey's contribution to this series, *Evaluation and Effective Public Management*. By focusing on key aspects of "results-oriented management" — evaluability assessment, performance measurement, evaluation design, outcome monitoring, implementation, and incentives — Wholey provides a valuable guide for action for those inside and outside of government who seek improvement in public programs and operations. Throughout his book, Wholey buttresses his analysis with vivid examples of results-oriented management at work in federal and state agencies and uses these examples to show how these management technologies help to solve the all-too-familiar problems government faces when trying to deliver programs that are at once efficient, effective, and responsible.

The readers of this book, indeed of the whole series, whether they are undergraduate students of public administration, those enrolled in a professional master's degree program, or people employed full time as public managers, should find the books uniformly readable, insightful, and useful. Readers should come to better understand and more fully appreciate the distinctive features of public management and organizations, and the difficulties in improving governmental performance in a democratic system that values accountability, equity, and rationality.

Charles H. Levine

# Preface

All of us want good government: as policymakers and managers, as government workers, as citizens and taxpayers. Yet government too often performs poorly, particularly in the eyes of the media and the public. Too often, government appears to be wasteful, ineffective, or unresponsive to public needs. While public needs continue to multiply in our increasingly complex society, public confidence in government has reached an all-time low and public-sector resources have been sharply reduced.

To compound the problem, government managers are burdened with an increasing multitude of process restrictions. Many of the government's "management-support" functions inhibit rather than promote effective service delivery.

At all levels, government is on a downward spiral of influence. Yet in many areas we need effective government action to protect the health, safety, and welfare of the general public and to meet the needs of elderly people and others who require special services.

As a result of my experience and the experience of others over the last twenty years, I believe that much more policy-level attention and analytical talent should go into activities designed to improve the management and performance of agencies and programs. In this book I suggest a general approach and specific ways in which government managers, policymakers, and analytical staff can reverse the downward spiral in government effectiveness; achieve demonstrable improvements in government management, performance, and results; and help restore public confidence in government.

A way of looking at and measuring the management effectiveness of government agencies is my message in the first chapter. Chapters 2 through 4 show how evaluators can produce preliminary evaluations of program designs and help build policy and management consensus on realistic, outcome-oriented objectives and performance indicators by which programs can be assessed and managed. These are followed by three chapters (5 through 7) in which I present relatively inexpensive methods that managers and policymakers can use to assess the performance and results of government programs. In Chapters 8 through 10, I suggest ways in which policymakers and staff offices can stimulate and reward demonstrable improvements in government management, performance, and results. To help bring the concepts to life at all levels of government, examples are provided throughout.

The evaluation and management strategies presented here have been developed and tested with the help of many friends and colleagues in the Department of Health, Education, and Welfare (now the Department of Health and Human Services) and at the Urban Institute over the last fifteen years.

Thanks are due especially to Richard Schmidt, a clear thinker and tower of strength in the Department and at the Institute; to Mark Abramson, John Heinberg, and Carol McHale, who played key roles in redirecting the Department's evaluation program; and to John Scanlon and Jay Bell, who have shown me the way so often.

In the Office of the Assistant Secretary for Planning and Evaluation, thanks are due to Hank Aaron, Ben Heineman, John Palmer, and Wray Smith, who provided the necessary top-level support; to Larry Beyna, John Daley, Jerry Haar, Bill Holland, Mike Jewell, Irene Monroe, Elsie O'Neal, Dave Pharis, Mary Pope, Vicki Schieber, Marian Solomon, Bruce Spitz, Martin Strosberg, John Van Kuren, and Ed Yates of the Office of Evaluation and Technical Analysis; and to our contractor colleagues at Applied Management Sciences, Consad Research Corporation, Granville Corporation, Macro Systems, System Sciences, and Urban Systems Research and Engineering.

At Department level, Joe Califano, Hale Champion, Tom McFee, Tom Morris, and Bryan Mitchell supported and encouraged the results-oriented management and management-oriented evaluation work described here. In the U.S. Office of Personnel Management, Scottie Campbell, Jule Sugarman, and Edie Goldenberg provided similar support.

Charles Levine suggested the book and provided helpful advice as it took shape. Mark Abramson, Jay Bell, Mike Hendricks, John Kirlin, John Scanlon, Richard Schmidt, and two anonymous reviewers provided very helpful comments on portions of the manuscript. Students at the University of Southern California and participants in training workshops provided useful reactions and insights as the material was developed.

On the home front, Midge again proved herself a wise adviser and counselor, Skef helped me through the difficult early days with the Apple, and Kate distinguished herself as a determined research assistant.

My thanks to one and all!

J.S.W.

# EVALUATION
# AND EFFECTIVE
# PUBLIC MANAGEMENT

# PART

# Effective
# Management

# 1

# Results-Oriented Management

## INTRODUCTION

The public always wants more services than it is willing to support through taxes; thus, tension always exists between "better services" and "lower taxes." In recent years, however, the public has more and more often been siding with those who would cut taxes and spending, regardless of impacts on services. Elections in the 1970s and early 1980s produced victory after victory for candidates promising less government and lower tax rates, while referenda and legislative actions resulted in a multitude of tax-limitation measures cutting the resources available to federal, state, and local governments.[1]

The late 1970s signaled growing dissatisfaction with government: witness Jimmy Carter's successful 1976 campaign for the presidency as a Washington outsider; California's 1978 adoption of Proposition 13, sharply reducing property taxes; and a variety of other limitations on taxation and government spending throughout the decade. In 1980 American voters selected as President another outsider, Ronald Reagan, who pledged to cut taxes and to reduce the burden of government. On the same day, voters in Massachusetts, the most liberal state in the union, adopted Proposition 2½, which greatly reduced taxes and government services. The popularity of Washington outsiders like Carter and Reagan, and of tax-limitation measures like Proposition 13 in California and Proposition 2½ in Massachusetts, is dramatic evidence of public loss of confidence in government.

3

And the people are not entirely wrong in their perceptions of government, for government is too often wasteful, ineffective, or unresponsive to public needs. Without the type of accountability that directs profit-making firms to seek out needs and to meet them efficiently, government agencies often appear as self-perpetuating bureaucracies primarily interested in growth, salaries, and benefits. Faced with example after example of inefficient, ineffective, or unresponsive government, the people are speaking; they are complaining of high taxes, poor services, and the harmful side effects of well-intended programs.

As government fails to demonstrate efficient response to public needs, elected and appointed policymakers lose confidence in career executives and managers. Correctly perceiving public unhappiness with government, higher-level policymakers are less willing to argue for the resources needed to provide effective services. Public alienation from government is currently expressing itself in strict limits on taxes, government expenditures, and government pay, travel, and data collection.

In *Management: Tasks, Responsibilities, Practices*, Peter Drucker notes that performance and results are exceptions in government agencies and other public-service institutions. Drucker's diagnosis is that government agencies and other public-service institutions tend to be misdirected because they are supported by budget allocations rather than being paid for results — and that such agencies therefore tend to fragment their resources by trying to please everyone. Failing to think through their objectives and to set priorities, government agencies and other public-service institutions tend to be ineffective. Generalizing from some of the rare exceptions (for example, the Bell Telephone System in the first half of the century and the Tennessee Valley Authority in the 1930s and 1940s), Drucker argues that government agencies and other public-service institutions should take the kinds of steps he calls "managing for performance" or "managing for performance and results." In this book we use an alternate term, *results-oriented management,* to identify the types of management activities that Drucker recommends: defining agency and program objectives by the outcomes to be achieved; setting priorities; defining qualitative and quantitative performance measures and performance targets; assessing performance and results; using performance information to improve performance and results; and identifying and abandoning unproductive activities.[2]

In principle, Drucker is on the right track; however, the realities of the government policymaking and management environment hinder progress in the directions he suggests. Program goals tend to be vague or unachievable; program performance is often hard to define and measure; political and bureaucratic constraints often make it difficult to use program performance information to improve program or agency performance.

This book presents approaches and methods that those in government can use to overcome problems in the policy and management environment and to carry through the activities recommended by Drucker. I suggest ways in which government managers, policymakers, and staff can improve government management, performance, and results; provide needed public services; communicate the value of government programs; and help rebuild public confidence in government.

Here the reader may find it helpful to consider two contrasting pictures of government management: (1) results-oriented management (outcome-oriented management); (2) process-oriented management.

Figure 1–1 outlines the structure of resource expenditures, program activities, program outcomes, information flows, and uses of information characterizing results-oriented management. Results-oriented managers establish realistic, measurable, outcome-oriented program objectives in terms of which they assess and manage their programs and report to higher policy levels (for example, to the chief executive or to legislative bodies).

By way of contrast, Figure 1–2 outlines the structure of resource expenditures, program activities, information flows, and uses of information characterizing the process-oriented management that is more typical of government. Here program objectives are limited to input and process objectives; programs are assessed and managed in terms of input and process objectives; and reports to policy levels are based on input and process data.

The keys to results-oriented management are (1) agreement on a set of program outcome objectives and outcome indicators in terms of which the program will be assessed and managed; (2) development of systems for assessing program performance in terms

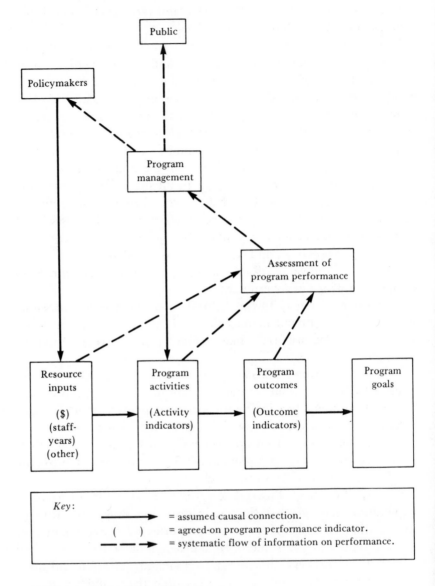

Figure 1-1 Results-Oriented Management

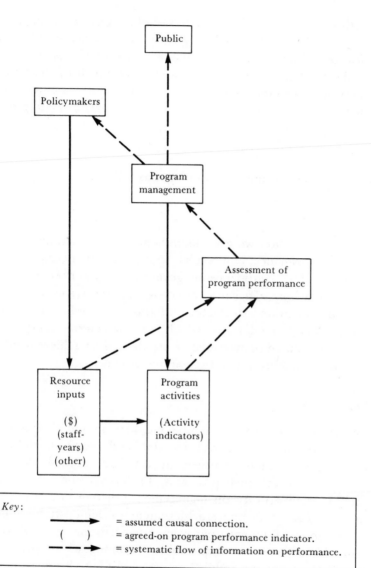

Figure 1-2  **Process-Oriented Management**

of those outcome objectives; (3) use of program outcome information to achieve improved program performance; and (4) communication of program performance and results to policy levels and to the public. We are all process-oriented much of the time. The question is whether and to what extent results-oriented management exists or should exist in government agencies and programs.

## The Central Argument

In summary, our line of reasoning is as follows:

### Assumptions

Across the nation we need improvements in government management, performance, and results, to meet public needs and to help restore public confidence in government. We need government programs whose efficiency, effectiveness, and responsiveness have been demonstrated to elected and appointed policymakers and to the public. Several steps, which we characterize collectively as "results-oriented management," are needed to achieve demonstrable improvements in government performance.

### Conclusions

Government managers and policymakers should therefore place priority on, and direct available staff and overhead resources to, the results-oriented management activities needed to produce demonstrably effective programs. Evaluators and other analysts should place priority on management-oriented evaluation activities designed to facilitate achievement of demonstrable improvements in government management, performance, and results.

In this chapter we explore the meaning of results-oriented management in the public sector, clarifying the concepts that underlie management approaches examined in the succeeding chapters. Here and in succeeding chapters, we suggest a spirit and a set of approaches designed for application in the constantly changing environments in which government managers work. The examples from federal, state, and local levels show the feasibility of achieving demonstrable improvements in government performance.

## Initial Assumptions and Definitions

*Across the nation we need improvements in government manage-
ment, performance, and results, to meet public needs and to
help restore public confidence in government. We need programs
whose efficiency, effectiveness, and responsiveness have been
demonstrated to elected and appointed policymakers and to the
public.*

We will use the terms *program, program performance, performance indicator,* and *demonstrably effective program* in the following senses.

A *program* is a set of resources and activities directed toward
one or more common goals, typically under the direction of one
manager or a management team. Under this definition, for example, the entire U.S. Public Health Service (PHS) can be thought
of as a program, as can the PHS Immunization Program (a collection of activities occurring in several different legislatively defined
programs), or the National Cancer Institute, or a research center
funded by the National Cancer Institute, or a research project
within such a center.

*Program performance* includes the resources expended on a
program, the program activities undertaken, and the outcomes and
impacts of program activities. In particular, as we use the term
here, program performance includes program outcomes and
impacts: progress toward program goals as well as positive and
negative side effects of the program. We sometimes use the alternate term *program performance and results* to remind readers of
our emphasis on program outcomes and impacts.

*Program performance indicators* specify the types of evidence
— qualitative or quantitative — that will be used to assess program
performance and results. (Performance indicators for the PHS
Immunization Program, for example, might include program costs,
amount of vaccine used, number of shots administered, and
number and percentage of children fully immunized.) Program
performance indicators include indicators of program productivity,
effectiveness, cost-effectiveness, quality, timeliness, and responsiveness. Program performance indicators may — and often do —
include indicators of important side effects of the program.

*Agreed-on performance indicators* are those performance indicators that the managers and policymakers in charge of a program have agreed to use to assess program performance and results. In this book we place special emphasis on the need for policy and management agreement on sets of specific program outcome indicators in terms of which programs are to be assessed and managed.

*Program performance targets* are levels of expected or improved program performance, stated in terms of agreed-on program performance indicators. We call program objectives or performance targets realistic (or plausible) if there is some likelihood that they will be achieved; unrealistic (implausible), if not. We might argue, for example, about whether "elimination of measles by 1990" is a realistic performance target for the PHS Immunization Program, given the likely availability of resources for that program.

A *demonstrably effective program* is a program for which (1) managers and relevant policymakers have agreed on a set of realistic, outcome-oriented program objectives, performance indicators, and performance targets in terms of which the program is to be assessed and managed; (2) managers have developed a system for assessing program performance and results in terms of those program objectives, performance indicators, and performance targets; (3) program performance has met or exceeded the agreed-on performance targets; and (4) management has communicated program performance to elected or appointed policymakers and to the public.

## Additional Assumptions and Definitions: A Results-Oriented Management Scale

*Several steps, which we characterize collectively as "results-oriented management," are needed to achieve demonstrable improvements in government performance.*

As we use the term here, *management* is the purposeful use of resources to achieve progress toward one or more goals. Although the term *administration* suggests the use of resources to create or maintain one or more intended activities, *management* suggests the use of resources to achieve intended outcomes related to agency/program goals.

In my view, government needs a special kind of management, results-oriented management, directed at producing demonstrable improvements in the performance and results of government agencies and programs. As we are using the term here, *results-oriented management* is the purposeful use of resources and information to achieve measurable progress toward program outcome objectives related to program goals. Results-oriented management includes several steps, which can be thought of as an ascending scale (see Table 1-1).[3]

At Level 0 on the "results-oriented management scale," policy-makers and managers have identified the programs for which a government organization is responsible, and identified the program managers responsible for those programs.

Level 1 is the key step. At Level 1, managers have defined and gotten policy-level agreement on the dimensions that will characterize program performance at a given time. At this level, program performance has been defined in terms of a set of realistic, results-oriented program objectives and a set of program performance indicators that appropriately reflect legislative intent, agency priorities, working-level realities, and resource constraints. (Program objectives and performance indicators will be outcome-oriented to the extent practicable. Program objectives may include negative side effects to be minimized.)

At Level 2, management has established a system for assessing program performance, and intra-program variations in performance, in terms of the agreed-on performance indicators. At Level 3, management has established realistic target levels of expected or improved program performance in terms of the agreed-on program objectives and program performance indicators. At Level 4, management has established a system for using information on program performance to stimulate improved program performance.

At Level 5, management has achieved efficient, effective program performance in terms of the agreed-on program objectives, performance indicators, and performance targets. At Level 6, management has communicated program performance and results (that is, has communicated the value of program activities) to policy levels and to the public. (When the program is an entire government or an entire agency, it may be necessary to eliminate harmful or low-priority subprograms in order to achieve and

**Table 1-1 Results-Oriented Management Scale**

Level 0: Policymakers and managers have defined the program (a set of resources and activities directed toward one or more common goals) and defined who is responsible for managing the program.

Level 1: Management has defined and gotten policy-level agreement on a set of realistic, results-oriented program objectives and a set of qualitative or quantitative program performance indicators in terms of which the program will be assessed and managed.[a]

Level 2: Management has established a system for assessing program performance, and intra-program variations in performance, in terms of the program objectives and performance indicators identified and agreed on at Level 1.

Level 3: Management has established and gotten policy-level agreement on realistic target levels of expected (or improved) program performance in terms of the program objectives identified at Level 1 and the measurement system established at Level 2.[b]

Level 4: Management has established a system for using information on program performance (and intra-program variations in performance) to stimulate improved program performance.

Level 5: Management has achieved efficient, effective program performance in terms of the performance targets established at Level 3.

Level 6: Management has communicated program performance and results to policy levels and to the public.

[a]The set of program objectives and program performance indicators will be outcome-oriented to the extent practicable and will become more outcome-oriented over time.
[b]Performance targets will be revised periodically to reflect past performance in the program or related programs and to reflect changes in policy-level commitments of resources and support.

demonstrate efficient, effective performance in the program itself.)[4]

At any given time, the set of program objectives and performance indicators used in managing a program will be results-oriented (outcome-oriented) to the extent practicable. Indicators of program productivity, quality and timeliness of service, effectiveness, and responsiveness will be included to the extent practicable. Program objectives, performance indicators, and systems for assessing program performance will be revised periodically to reflect changes in policy, changes in resources available, changes in management priorities, and changes in availability of appropriate program performance indicators. Management typically will become more results-oriented in time, as relevant outcome objectives are established and appropriate outcome indicators are identified.

## Conclusion 1: Management Priorities

*Government managers and policymakers should therefore place priority on, and direct available staff and overhead resources to, results-oriented management activities needed to produce demonstrably effective programs.*

Government managers and policymakers should take responsibility for producing demonstrably effective programs. In particular, managers should take responsibility for achieving policy and management agreement on sets of results-oriented program objectives, performance indicators, and performance targets — and take responsibility for assessing and reporting on expected and actual program performance and results.

If anticipated or actual program results continue to be unacceptable, managers and policymakers should change program objectives or redirect resources to improve program, agency, and government efficiency and effectiveness. In some cases, this will mean phasing out unproductive agency/program activities.

## Conclusion 2: Evaluation Priorities

*Evaluators and other analysts should place priority on management-oriented evaluation activities designed to facilitate achievement of demonstrable improvements in government management, performance, and results.*

Past evaluation activities usually have not helped managers to produce more effective programs. Most evaluations have been directed at policy and budget decisions, or at production of knowledge for its own sake.

If our analysis is correct, evaluators — as well as policy analysts, management analysts, budget analysts, personnel analysts, auditors, and other overhead staff — should instead place priority on management-oriented evaluation activities designed to produce the following: (1) policy and management agreement on sets of realistic, results-oriented program objectives and performance indicators; (2) evidence on program performance in terms of those objectives and performance indicators; and (3) demonstrable improvements in program performance and results. Management-oriented evaluation includes six types of activity intended to stimulate and support results-oriented management:

1. Working with program managers, policymakers, those delivering services, and relevant interest groups to identify program goals and agency priorities; to diagnose program potential; to get policy and management agreements defining the sets of program objectives and program performance indicators that will be used in assessing program performance and results; and to identify options for improving program and agency performance.
2. Developing systems for assessing program performance in terms of agreed-on program objectives and performance indicators.
3. Working with managers and policymakers to establish realistic target levels of expected or improved program performance, in terms of agreed-on program objectives and performance indicators.
4. Developing systems for using information on program performance, and intra-program variations in performance, to stimulate and reward improvements in program and agency performance and results.
5. Assessing program performance and results in terms of agreed-on program objectives, performance indicators, and performance targets; in particular, documenting program performance and intra-program variations in performance, comparing program performance with prior or expected performance, documenting how especially good performance is achieved, and identifying factors inhibiting better program performance.

6. Communicating program performance to policy levels and to the public.

These activities are the focus of the succeeding chapters.

## PROBLEMS AND SOLUTIONS

Government managers are ambivalent about managing for results. Though interested in demonstrating success, they are uneasy about being held accountable for poor organizational performance. In the typical situation in which they do not have complete control over resources, government managers are often unwilling to take the steps needed to achieve demonstrable improvements in organizational performance and results.

Though "results-oriented management" may sound fine in theory, there are severe problems in achieving it in practice: problems in getting agreement on what "good performance" means in a program or organization; lack of management authority over resources; management unwillingness to take responsibility for results; problems in getting information on program performance; and problems in motivating improved program performance. If these problems did not exist, this book and many other management aids would be unnecessary. The problems do exist. These approaches were developed to help overcome these problems.

### Problems in Getting Agreement
### on What "Good Performance" Means
### in a Given Program or Organization

Government programs operate in complex political environments, pushed and pulled in many directions by legislative bodies and by a multitude of funding and regulatory organizations, grantees, and interest groups. Organizations at different levels tend to have different goals for the same program; conflicting or competing goals are often found even within the same organization.

In local, regional, and federal government, I have seen clear examples of such conflicts: conflicts among housing, economic development, and public finance goals in local government; conflicts between equity and simplicity in metropolitan area subway and bus fares; conflicts between efficiency and service goals in the hospice movement. Table 1-2 suggests goal conflicts that have existed in federally funded mental health programs. You have, I am sure, come across similar goal conflicts.

Given such conflicts, there will always be difficulties in achieving policy and management agreement on the sets of program objectives and program performance indicators that characterize "good performance" in a given program. Program goals tend to be vague, conflicting, and often unrealistic. In a political environment many actors will influence program funding and program policies; the objectives and priorities of important actors will vary over time; and there will always be negative consequences if managers and policymakers attempt to give priority to some objectives.

In this book, I suggest three ways of overcoming these difficulties: involvement of important actors in building a policy and management consensus on the most important program objectives and performance indicators; explicit use of multiple objectives and multiple performance indicators in defining "good performance"; and use of qualitative as well as quantitative indicators to capture the nuances of good program performance.

Evaluability assessment (Chapters 2-4) provides managers and policymakers with a process for setting realistic, measurable objectives related to interest group needs, legislative goals, agency priorities, working-level realities, and resource constraints.

Policy and management use of multiple program objectives and performance indicators in defining "good performance" — and periodic revision of program objectives and performance indicators — reflects the reality of program operations in a political environment. Grounding the set of program objectives and performance indicators in legislative goals and working-level reality gives some stability to the set of program objectives, which otherwise might shift violently as policymakers come and go.

The evaluators' use of qualitative as well as quantitative performance indicators keeps the evaluation process closer to reality and closer to managers' and policymakers' interests. Program reality and the program environment are too complicated to be captured in a few numbers; and higher-level managers and policymakers are accustomed to using qualitative as well as quantitative data.

**Table 1-2   Competing and Conflicting Goals: Hypothetical Priorities of Important Actors in Mental Health Programs[a]**

| Goals | Federal government | | | State government | Local government | Grantee | Client |
|---|---|---|---|---|---|---|---|
| | Congress | OMB | HHS | | | | |
| 1. Deinstitutionalizing mental patients | M | | A | A | Z | | |
| 2. Serving deinstitutionalized patients | | | M | | A | | |
| 3. Effective services | | | M | M | | M | A |
| 4. Cost-effectiveness | | | | | | | |
| 5. Serving the elderly | A | | A | | | | |
| 6. Serving minorities | M | | A | | | | |
| 7. Organizational survival | | | | | | A | |
| 8. Expanding services | | Z | M | | | M | |
| 9. EEO | M | | M | | | | |
| 10. Spending current appropriation | | Z | A | | | A | |
| 11. Restraining spending | M | A | Z | | | Z | |
| 12. Deregulation | | M | | | | | |
| 13. Reducing paperwork | M | M | | | | | |
| 14. Productivity | | | | | | | |
| 15. Maximizing third-party reimbursements | M | | M | | | A | |
| 16. Consumer satisfaction | | | | | | M | M |

a"A" indicates a high-priority goal; "M," medium priority; "Z," opposition to the goal.

## Lack of Authority over Resources

An increasing problem in recent years has been the geometric growth in constraints on public managers. At a 1980 Federal Executive Institute seminar I attended with top career executives from throughout the federal government, for example, this was a constant theme:

> The capacity to manage in the federal government — from the point of view of the manager — has been significantly reduced. This has happened over time in a number of ways, and for a variety of reasons:
>
> 1. The diffusion of power and increasing variety and complexity of organizations which share the policy/decision making authority.
> 2. The growth of categorical interests (one-issue clientele groups, single-minded lobbyists, narrow Congressional subcommittee jurisdictions, etc.). . . .
> 4. The growth of outside overlays of public policy which managers are required to implement (such things as Buy American, air pollution, small business and minority business development, noise abatement, rural development, urban revitalization, historic preservation, clear water protection, equal employment practices . . . and even control of inflation). . . .
> 6. The growing complexity, time delays and hassling which burden our major management systems—the budget, the procurement process, the major computer acquisition process, the personnel system and even obtaining office space and normal office equipment. . . .[5]

Government "managers" often do not see themselves as having power or authority. In the political environment in which government managers operate, it is impossible for managers to achieve results by giving orders. Management becomes a matter of influencing resources and activities that one does not control.

The best managers, those who know what they are trying to accomplish, are able to create the cooperation needed to achieve progress toward important objectives. Building a consensus on important objectives gives direction to the enterprise; support from higher management and policy levels will usually be needed as well.

## Unwillingness to Take Responsibility for Results

The central problem in results-oriented management relates to managers' unwillingness to take responsibility for program results, given the reality that their authority extends (at best) only as far as control over program activities. Much of government management is — and has to be — process-oriented, responding to legislative and public inquiries within a reasonable time, administering program activities in accord with the law and agency regulations, getting grants out to eligible recipients, and meeting the demands of higher management and policy levels. Agreement on intended results will be hampered by uncertainty over availability of resources and by uncertainty over cause-and-effect relationships among program activities and intended program outcomes.

But government programs exist to achieve results!

The keys to success in getting managers to take responsibility for program results appear to lie in three activities that are the focus of this book: (1) providing managers with information on the expectations and concerns of legislative bodies, higher-level policymakers, those delivering services in the program, and important interest groups (Chapters 2-4); (2) providing managers with information on their programs' potential for effective performance (Chapters 2-7); and (3) providing managers with positive incentives to "stretch" toward achievement of program results — outcomes and impacts — that lie beyond compliance with process requirements (Chapter 9). From the points of view of managers and policymakers, the key notion is that of management "ability to influence," rather than "control," as the criterion in selecting the results for which managers are asked to take responsibility. To rebuild public confidence in government, government managers and policymakers must achieve demonstrable improvements in the results of public programs.

## Problems in Getting Information
## on Program Performance

All the problems we are discussing are interrelated. Unless there is a consensus on the objectives and performance indicators in terms of which a program is to be assessed and managed, it is unlikely that valid program-performance information will be obtainable. Unless the consensus extends to outcome objectives and outcome indicators, it is unlikely that valid information will be obtained on program results.

In this book I suggest how managers, policymakers, and those at working levels can come to agreement on the types of information required to demonstrate effective program performance and results (Chapters 2-4). I also show how managers can assess program performance and results at reasonable costs in staff time, dollars, and goodwill (Chapters 5-7).

## Problems in Motivating Improved Performance

Individual managers can and do manage for results. When managers wish to manage for results, evaluators can help with the management-oriented evaluation methods presented in Chapters 2-7. But results-oriented management is comparatively rare in government because of the accumulation of disincentives mentioned earlier.

What can be done to stimulate results-oriented management and improved program performance?

To achieve consistent progress in results-oriented management, government needs to change the existing incentive systems. Government policymakers and managers can use either tangible incentives (such as support for discretionary funds in proposed budgets, authority to maintain or increase numbers of staff, cash bonuses, or merit pay) or intangible incentives (such as relaxation of constraints, delegation of authority, personal recognition, or public recognition). In a number of the examples in this chapter, we will see the use of incentive schemes to stimulate improved organizational performance.

In recent years, many government agencies have tested incentive systems to motivate better management and performance. There are some indications that, in government, intangible incentives may be more important than financial incentives. I have found that government managers are enthusiastic, for example, over incentives involving "relaxation of constraints" and "delegation of authority."

Though the way to solutions is far from clear, it is clear that solutions are needed. In Chapter 9, we will explore the creation of incentives designed to motivate improved government management, performance, and results.

## EXAMPLES OF RESULTS-ORIENTED MANAGEMENT

Like effective management in general, results-oriented management requires both a spirit and a systematic approach. This section presents examples of results-oriented management at federal, state, and local levels. In these examples, we will use the results-oriented management scale shown in Table 1-1. Progress along the scale indicates that management is carrying out the "results-oriented management" activities: achieving policy and management agreement on sets of realistic, results-oriented program objectives and performance indicators, establishing systems for assessing program performance and results, and so on.

### Community Health Services

In the Department of Health and Human Services (HHS), before a block-grant "reform" proposed by the Reagan administration, the Bureau of Community Health Services stood out as one of the best-managed programs. The bureau gave direction to HHS regional office administration of grant-in-aid programs totaling hundreds of millions of dollars annually. Among the bureau's performance targets, for example, was that of immunizing at least 90 percent of children aged twenty-four to twenty-seven months.

Using program objectives, performance indicators, and performance targets that had been developed with the participation of regional offices and grantees over a four-year period,[6] the bureau allocated staff and grant funds in ways that stimulated efficient, effective program performance. The bureau allocated additional staff and grant funds to high-performing regions; regional offices allocated additional grant funds to high-performing projects. On the results-oriented management scale (Table 1-1), the bureau director, Dr. Edward D. Martin, and the bureau appeared to rate a Level 5.

Results-oriented management is no panacea, however. Strong political tides can overwhelm even the best-managed program. The bureau apparently was unsuccessful in communicating its effective performance to Reagan administration policymakers or to the members of the 97th Congress. In the Omnibus Budget Reconciliation Act of 1981, P. L. 97-35, most of the bureau's program was folded into a system of health services block grants to the states.

## Head Start

The national Head Start program had never been known as one of the leaders in results-oriented management. Early evaluations showed that policymakers had set unrealistic expectations for Head Start impact;[7] later management efforts were focused on dozens of process objectives that gave little sense of direction to the program.[8]

From 1978 to 1980, however, under the influence of Joseph A. Califano, Jr., former Secretary of Health, Education, and Welfare, Head Start moved to Level 3 on the results-oriented management scale. In 1978, with the help of staff from the Office of the Secretary, Head Start established a set of thirteen program performance indicators in terms of which local, regional, and national Head Start performance would be assessed. The Head Start performance indicators included, for example, number and percentage of children completing all required immunizations, and number and percentage of children receiving needed medical and dental treatment. Early in 1979, after discussing the indicators with regional office staff and grantee representatives, Head Start management adapted existing information systems, installed a new on-site monitoring system on a trial basis, and began collecting information in terms of the agreed-on performance indicators. By 1980, using baseline data on local, regional, and national performance in 1978-1979 and 1979-1980, and using inputs from regional offices, Head Start management had established semiannual and annual target levels of expected 1980-1981 program performance in terms of the performance indicators.

Further work was undertaken on possible new Head Start performance indicators, to better measure certain dimensions of program performance (for example, indicators of impact on Head Start parents' lives and possible indicators of Head Start influence on children's subsequent progress in elementary school).

By the end of 1980, Head Start managers were moving toward Level 4 on the results-oriented management scale, as they planned to allocate technical assistance resources to improve grantee performance in terms of the agreed-on performance indicators and performance targets.

## Student Loans

Between 1977 and 1979, HEW Secretary Joseph A. Califano, Jr., and Leo Kornfeld, Deputy Commissioner of Education, redirected the previously troubled and politically vulnerable Guaranteed Student Loan Program. Secretary Califano considered it imperative that HEW restore the public's confidence by efficient management of social programs:

> Ours is the challenge of expressing compassion — but compassion disciplined by competence; we must be as wise as we are caring.
> Nothing less will work, in a time of limited resources. Nothing else will do, if we are to restore people's confidence in their government. That is why HEW has recently embarked on an historic effort to increase the efficiency of its programs; to root out fraud and abuse; to streamline the machinery of government.[9]

Secretary Califano and Commissioner Kornfeld set clear objectives for the student loan program — to lower the default rate, to move loans from default to repayment status, to collect money due the government — and they set quarterly and annual targets for improved performance. Kornfeld followed up by communicating these objectives to HEW regional offices and establishing incentive systems under which HEW staff members could compete for cash incentives and other awards in a "Collection Olympics." By 1979 Califano and Kornfeld were able to report movement of more than eighty thousand federally insured loans from default to repayment status. Congress responded to this Level 6 performance by maintaining and greatly expanding the student loan program.[10]

## Harlem Valley Psychiatric Center

Even in the "hard-to-measure" mental health arena, Dr. Yoosuf Haveliwala, director of the Harlem Valley Psychiatric Center (a state institution in rural Wingdale, New York), was able to produce efficient, effective services by establishing clear, results-oriented objectives; establishing systems for assessing the performance and results achieved by units within the center; establishing target levels for improved performance; and creating incentives for improved organizational performance in terms of agreed-on objectives, performance indicators, and performance targets. In *From State Hos-*

*pital to Psychiatric Center,* Professor Murray Levine presents an exciting case study of Dr. Haveliwala's efforts, which between 1974 and 1977 transformed a state mental hospital primarily serving its 1,826 inpatients into a psychiatric center providing an extensive array of excellent services to 590 inpatients and 2,478 outpatients.[11]

The situation Dr. Haveliwala faced in 1974 was that faced by many government managers in the 1980s: Dr. Haveliwala took over an organization whose future was in doubt. As had happened throughout the country, higher-level policymakers in the state legislature and the state Department of Mental Hygiene had decided that mental patients should be returned to the community whenever possible. The Harlem Valley mental hospital was threatened with closing within a few years.[12]

Dr. Haveliwala took seriously the department's twin goals of deinstitutionalization and provision of needed care in the community. Upon becoming director, he immediately established very clear objectives for the center: rapid reduction of the inpatient census, appropriate placements in the community, development of community-based services, and high-quality care for all patients in the hospital and in the community. Contrary to the practice of other state hospitals, the Harlem Valley Psychiatric Center followed through on deinstitutionalization by creating needed services at community level, redirecting resources from inpatient care to outpatient care as the inpatient census fell.[13]

For assessing the performance of the center and of organizational units within the center, Dr. Haveliwala used at least seven different systems: program evaluation, quality assurance, quality-care, epidemiological studies, research studies, a community placement review committee, and a program review committee. Besides the analytical staff involved full time in most of these assessment systems, staff from throughout the center helped to assess the performance of other units, using what Dr. Haveliwala considered would otherwise have been slack time.[14]

Dr. Haveliwala involved managers in establishing objectives for their units. "Line" units in charge of patients were assessed in terms of qualitative and quantitative performance indicators, such as number of inpatients, quality of inpatient services, adequacy of medical records, length of stay, number of inpatients to be placed in community settings, number of inpatients actually placed in community settings, quality and appropriateness of placements in the community, number of discharged patients followed in outpatient settings, and current status of discharged patients. "Staff" units were assessed in terms of their responsiveness in providing needed services. Data on organizational performance were used in identifying problems, in initiating corrective actions, and in reallocating resources. The performance of all units was well publicized throughout — and beyond — the center.[15]

Dr. Haveliwala used his authority to reassign responsibilities and an array of intangible incentives to motivate improved individual and organizational performance. (Dr. Haveliwala was operating in a strict civil service system, where changes in pay or grade came slowly.) If a line unit proved capable, for example, it would gain responsibilities and staff, while the responsibilities of other units were readjusted. If a line manager or staff member performed well, he or she might be rewarded by use of "acting" titles with greater responsibilities, entry into the director's inner circle, promotion, more flexible working hours, or availability of subsidized housing. If a line or staff unit performed particularly well, its staff might be rewarded with challenging new projects, educational leave, trips to conventions, certificates of improvement, an informal meeting with the director, or other intangible rewards.[16]

By the end of a three-year period, the Harlem Valley Psychiatric Center had achieved dramatic progress toward its objectives — as attested to by outside reviews — while simultaneously reducing costs from $19.5 million to $15.2 million.[17] Its demonstrable improvements in performance and results, and the center's communication of those results to policy levels and to the public, merit Harlem Valley a Level 6 rating on the results-oriented management scale.

## Sunnyvale City Government

For years before "productivity" became a fashionable buzzword, John Dever, city manager of Sunnyvale, California, produced efficient, effective local services using a management system that included all the elements characterizing results-oriented management: management by outputs and results; measurement of program quality and citizen satisfaction; management use of information on progress toward goals and objectives; and communication with citizens on needs and on results achieved.[18] Based on the information available to me, including an inspiring face-to-face meeting in which Dever explained his management system, John Dever and the Sunnyvale city government appear to rate a Level 6 on the results-oriented management scale.

## Comparing Relative Performance in Results-Oriented Management

In addition to being able to assess management and performance in a single program and to track performance changes over time, the results-oriented management scale is also useful in comparing the relative performance of managers responsible for different programs and in prescribing steps managers would have to take to demonstrate improved management and improved program performance. Table 1-3, for example, summarizes the management status of the five programs discussed. Like Stafford Beer's measures of productivity and latency, the results-oriented management scale provides a common metric that can be used to assess and

Table 1-3 Progress in Results-Oriented Management: Selected Cases[a]

| Program | Level 0 | Level 1 | Level 2 | Level 3 | Level 4 | Level 5 | Level 6 |
|---|---|---|---|---|---|---|---|
| 1. Community Health Services (1980) | X | X | X | X | X | X | |
| 2. Head Start (1980) | X | X | X | X | | | |
| 3. Guaranteed Student Loan Program (1979) | X | X | X | X | X | X | X |
| 4. Harlem Valley Psychiatric Center (1977) | X | X | X | X | X | X | X |
| 5. Sunnyvale, California (1970s) | X | X | X | X | X | X | X |

[a]Performance levels are defined in Table 1-1. "X" indicates that the program has attained a given performance level.

communicate the relative performance of different managers and different organizations.[19]

In 1980, as a part of the planning for an evaluation of the impact of civil service reform, I tested an earlier version of the results-oriented management scale on approximately twenty programs in the Health Resources Administration (HRA), one of the six agencies then constituting the U.S. Public Health Service. The test required (1) review of several sets of documents (for example, evaluation plans, performance appraisal plans for HRA managers, and MBO materials); (2) interviews with five high-level managers in the Health Resources Administration (the administrator, an associate administrator, and the three bureau chiefs); and (3) questionnaires sent to Department of Health and Human Services, Public Health Service, and Health Resources Administration analysts thought to be familiar with HRA programs. Those interviewed and those responding to the questionnaire were asked to rate the HRA programs on the results-oriented management scale. On the bases of these responses and the documents, I then rated the HRA programs on the results-oriented management scale (see Table 1-4).

The results of the test were as follows:

1. Relatively few HRA programs had fully attained Level 1 (agreement on a set of realistic, results-oriented program objectives in terms of which the program would be assessed and managed).
2. In the judgment of HRA managers, most HRA programs had partially attained Level 1. In many cases, these judgments were based on managers' agreements on process objectives and activity indicators.
3. Policy analysts and evaluators who responded tended to assign lower ratings than did managers.
4. There was one suggestion that it might be useful to subdivide Levels 1 and 2. (A division of Levels 1 and 2 into process objectives and outcome objectives has some appeal. Alternatively, a tougher standard could be employed in using the results-oriented management scale, by refusing to credit even partial attainment of Level 1 in the absence of agreement on appropriate outcome objectives and outcome indicators.)[20]

The test was sufficiently successful to encourage the Department

Table 1-4 Health Resources Administration Programs: Performance Levels Attained (October 1980)[a]

| Program | Level 1 | Level 2 | Level 3 | Level 5 |
|---|---|---|---|---|
| 1. Health facilities: Construction and loan guarantees | X | Y | Y | |
| 2. Health facilities: Conversion and closure[b] | | | | |
| 3. Health facilities: Compliance | Y | Y | Y | |
| 4. Health facilities: Energy programs | Y | Y | Y | |
| 5. Health planning | X | Y | Y | |
| 6. Dental Health Education | Y | | | |
| 7. Public health and health administration | Y | | | |
| 8. Allied health | | | | |
| 9. Health professions: Institutional support | X | X | | |
| 10. Health professions: Student aid | Y | | | |
| 11. National Health Service Corps scholarships | Y | Y | Y | Y |
| 12. Nursing: Institutional assistance | X | X | | |
| 13. Nursing: Student assistance | Y | | | |

to use the results-oriented management scale in evaluation of the impact of civil service reform (see Chapter 3).

## CONCLUSION

In the 1980s and beyond, governments at all levels face a dangerous loss of public confidence.

Government managers face severe resource constraints, changes in goals and priorities, and constraints on their authority and ability to manage.

Still, the problems are there. In our increasingly urbanized, increasingly interconnected society, many problems can be solved

Table 1-4   (Continued)

| Program | Level 1 | Level 2 | Level 3 | Level 5 |
|---|---|---|---|---|
| 14. Family medicine residencies and training | Y | | | |
| 15. Family medicine departments | Y | | | |
| 16. General internal medicine and pediatrics | Y | | | |
| 17. Physician assistants | Y | | | |
| 18. Health professions educational improvement and development projects | Y | | | |
| 19. Area Health Education Centers | X | Y | | |
| 20. Emergency medical training | Y | | | |
| 21. Health professions: Analytical studies and reports[b] | | | | |
| 22. Insured loans to graduate students in health professions[b] | | | | |
| 23. Graduate Medical Education National Advisory Committee | X | X | X | Y |
| 24. Disadvantaged assistance | X | Y | Y | Y |

[a]Performance levels are defined in Table 1-1. "X" indicates that the program has attained a given performance level; "Y," partial achievement of a performance level.
[b]Program 2 was not rated because the program had not yet been funded. Programs 21 and 22 were not rated because inadequate information was available.

only by government action. To promote the general welfare and to meet the special needs of elderly and disadvantaged people, government must act effectively.

Most government programs, including programs now being cut back as tax rates are reduced, were created to respond to real public needs. In many areas (such as national defense, law enforcement, transportation, health care and preventive health services, education, and income security for retired people and others in need), there is a consensus that government action is needed. In these areas at least — areas that cover most government expenditures — ineffective government has dangerous implications for us all.

The spirit of this book is that the management challenge of the

1980s must and can be met. In the 1980s and for the rest of this century, the product line of government managers and policy-makers must be demonstrably effective programs — programs that are demonstrably responsive to public needs.

Implicit in the notions of results-oriented management and demonstrably effective programs are four ideas: agreement on what effective performance means in a given agency or program; achievement of effective program performance; production of credible information documenting the key dimensions of program performance and results; and communication of program performance and results to policy levels and to the public. In Chapters 2–4 we will examine one way in which policy and management agreement can be achieved on sets of program objectives and performance indicators in terms of which programs are to be assessed and managed. Succeeding chapters will explore approaches for documenting program performance and for using program performance information to stimulate demonstrable improvements in program performance and results. These approaches are intended to help managers, policymakers, and analytical staffs produce demonstrably effective programs in the political and bureaucratic environments in which they and their programs operate.

Given the extent of public cynicism about government, production of demonstrable improvements in government performance is likely to require the efforts of policymakers, managers, and program staffs; of policy and management-support units like the U.S. Office of Management and Budget, the Office of Personnel Management, the General Accounting Office, and their counterparts in individual agencies and at other levels of government; and of individuals and public-interest groups outside government. If you're not part of the solution, you're part of the problem!

## NOTES TO CHAPTER 1

1. This chapter extends a line of argument I advanced in "Using Evaluation to Improve Program Performance," in Robert A. Levine and others, eds., *Evaluation Research and Practice: Comparative and International Perspectives* (Beverly Hills, Calif.: Sage Publications, 1981), pp. 92–106, and in Howard E. Freeman and Marian A. Solomon, eds., *Evaluation Studies Review Annual*, vol. 6 (Beverly Hills, Calif.: Sage Publications, 1981), pp. 55–69; and in

"Results Oriented Management: Integrating Evaluation and Organizational Performance Incentives," in Gerald J. Stahler and William R. Tash, eds., *Innovative Approaches to Mental Health Evaluation* (New York: Academic Press, 1982), pp. 255–275. I am grateful to those who have commented on these and other writings on results-oriented management, especially James Bell, John Scanlon, Richard Schmidt, Mark Abramson, Luis Cubillos, Jerry Haar, Harry Hatry, Michael Jewell, Murray Levine, Carol McHale, Alfred Schainblatt, Steven Scharfstein, Warren Schmidt, Carol Weiss, Helen J. Wholey, Margaret Wholey, and J. Richard Woy. James Bell, Charles Levine, and two anonymous reviewers provided very helpful comments on drafts of this and later chapters.

Harry Havens of the U.S. General Accounting Office has written along somewhat parallel lines, for example, in his paper, "The Role of Program Evaluation in Public Management," *Public Administration Review,* vol. 41, no. 4 (July/August 1981), pp. 480–485.

2.  Peter F. Drucker, *Management: Tasks, Responsibilities, Practices* (New York: Harper and Row, 1974), pp. 137–166.

3.  Richard Schmidt, Mark Abramson, and I developed this scale as part of efforts to redirect evaluation in the U. S. Department of Health and Human Services between 1978 and 1980.

4.  I thank Luis Cubillos, a former student at the University of Southern California's Washington Public Affairs Center, for stressing this point (personal communication). In this case the agency subprograms would be "programs" in the usual sense. Cubillos emphasized the fact that not all programs are worth being continued and improved, as application of a Planning-Programming-Budgeting (PPB) or Zero-Base Budgeting (ZBB) approach could reveal.

5.  Charles F. Bingman and Frank P. Sherwood, eds., *Management Improvement Agenda for the Eighties* (Charlottesville, Va.: U.S. Office of Personnel Management, Federal Executive Institute, FEI B-26, 1981), p. 1.

6.  See Heather Keppler-Seid, Charles Windle, and J. Richard Woy, "Performance Measures for Mental Health Programs: Something Better, Something Worse, or More of the Same?" *Community Mental Health Journal,* vol. 16, no. 3 (1980), pp. 217–234.

7.  See Walter Williams and John W. Evans, "The Politics of Evaluation: The Case of Head Start," *Annals of the American Academy of Political and Social Science,* September 1969.

8.  See the discussion of the Head Start program in Chapter 6.

9.  Joseph A. Califano, Jr., Secretary of Health, Education, and Welfare, "Remarks at the Opening Ceremonies, HEW's 25th Anniversary Celebration," Washington, D.C., May 23, 1978.

10.  See Joseph A. Califano, Jr., Secretary of Health, Education, and Welfare, "Memorandum for the Employees of the Department of Health, Education, and Welfare," Washington, D.C., July 26, 1979; and Phil Gailey, "HEW 'Olympians' Vie in Chasing Defaulters," *Washington Star,* February 8, 1979.

11.  Murray Levine, *From State Hospital to Psychiatric Center* (Lexington, Mass.: D. C. Heath and Company, 1980), pp. 15–17.

12. Ibid., p. 15.

13. Ibid., pp. 81–91.

14. Ibid., pp. 61–73.

15. Ibid., pp. 57–73.

16. Ibid., pp. 43–44 and 57–59.

17. Ibid., pp. 15–20 and 87.

18. See "Case Study in Government Productivity: Sunnyvale" (Peat, Marwick, Mitchell and Company, *World*, Autumn 1976). As a results-oriented manager, I found John Dever even more impressive in person.

19. Beer defines *productivity* as the ratio of actual performance to what could be done with existing resources under existing conditions. *Latency* is the ratio of what could be done with existing resources, under existing conditions, to what is already known to be feasible if resources were developed and constraints were removed. See Stafford Beer, *The Brain of the Firm*, 2d ed. (New York: Wiley, 1981), pp. 162–166; and Stafford Beer, *The Heart of the Enterprise* (New York: Wiley, 1979), pp. 290–299.

20. This account is based on Memorandum from Joe Wholey, "Civil Service Reform Evaluation: Test of Results-Oriented Management Scale in HRA," Office of the Secretary of Health and Human Services, November 17, 1980.

# PART

# Getting Agreement on Realistic, Results-Oriented Objectives and Performance Indicators

# 2

# Evaluability
# Assessment

## INTRODUCTION

In our first chapter we explored the notion of results-oriented
management: management directed at producing demonstrable
progress toward a specific set of realistic, measurable, outcome-
oriented program objectives. In this chapter we review the development of a powerful, relatively inexpensive tool for evaluation
known as *evaluability assessment* (or *exploratory evaluation*).
Evaluability assessment answers the question, not whether a program can be evaluated (every program can be evaluated), but
whether the program is ready to be managed for results, what
changes are needed to allow results-oriented management, and
whether evaluation is likely to contribute to improved program
performance. Originally developed as a preevaluation approach
aimed at determining if programs were ready for useful evaluation,
evaluability assessment has emerged as an evaluation tool in its
own right.[1]

Evaluability assessment is appropriate when there is policy or
management interest in improving program performance and a
willingness to invest in monitoring or evaluation — but policy and
management decisions have not been made defining program performance in terms of a specific set of realistic, measurable,
outcome-oriented program objectives. Evaluability assessment may
be conducted as a separate process or built in as the initial step in
a larger evaluation.

Evaluability assessment documents and clarifies program intent from the points of view of key actors in and around the program; it explores  program reality in order to clarify the plausibility of program objectives and the feasibility of performance measurement; and it helps develop policy and management consensus on desirable changes in program resources, activities, objectives, or the collection and use of program performance information.

Evaluability assessment is intended to help managers and policymakers to select sets of realistic, results-oriented program objectives and program performance indicators in terms of which they will assess and manage their programs, thus moving their programs to Level 1 on the results-oriented management scale introduced in Chapter 1 (Table 1-1). In many cases, evaluability assessment provides information that helps managers to introduce program changes likely to achieve improved program performance — or to communicate more clearly the value of existing program activities.

In this chapter we discuss the need for, and origin of, evaluability assessment; describe the evaluability assessment process and products; and present a simple example of this evaluation approach. In Chapters 3 and 4, we further explore evaluability assessment, presenting more complex examples of evaluability assessment process, products, and uses.

## PROBLEMS INHIBITING RESULTS-ORIENTED MANAGEMENT AND USEFUL PROGRAM EVALUATION

Results-oriented management is difficult to achieve in organizations not motivated by profit or return on investment, particularly when resources and program activities are controlled at levels far removed from the delivery of services. As we noted in Chapter 1, large public and nonprofit organizations are plagued by problems of inefficiency, ineffectiveness, unresponsiveness, and lack of purposeful activity directed toward common ends. Such organizations also tend to find it difficult to communicate the value of their activities.

Evaluability assessment helps those in charge of public programs to overcome five problems that inhibit results-oriented management and useful program evaluation. These problems are: (1) lack of agreement on program objectives and information priorities;

(2) implausibility of program objectives; (3) unavailability of relevant information on program performance; (4) management inability or unwillingness to act on the basis of program performance information; (5) management inability to communicate the value of program activities. We will now consider each of these problems.

## Lack of Agreement on Program Objectives and Information Priorities

In the absence of policy and management agreement on program objectives and information priorities, those designing evaluations tend to develop their own pictures of policy and management information needs, usually focusing on "rhetorical" program impact objectives suggested by authorizing legislation or the interests of the evaluators. Those designing management systems, on the other hand, tend to focus on input and process.

Born and sustained in compromise, most public programs have a large number of objectives—input objectives, process objectives, outcome objectives, and impact objectives — whose significance and relative importance can be assessed only with the help of managers and policymakers. Evaluability assessment helps those in charge of public programs to sort through the competing objectives of policymakers, managers, those delivering services in the program, those served by the program, and relevant interest groups. Using evaluability assessment, those in charge are often able to come to agreement on a set of program objectives and performance indicators in terms of which the program will be assessed and managed. (Program objectives and performance indicators can be changed as policy and management priorities change, as more is learned about the likelihood of effective program performance, and as relevant program performance measures are developed.)

## Implausibility of Program Objectives

Policymakers, higher-level managers, and evaluators are often guilty of attempting to hold programs accountable for progress toward objectives that are unrealistic because of resource constraints, insufficient time to demonstrate impact, or lack of knowledge indicating how objectives could be achieved.

Evaluability assessment helps those in charge of public programs to examine the plausibility of alternative sets of objectives before deciding on the sets of objectives in terms of which the program will be held accountable. If program objectives appear to be unrealistic, those in charge can consider changing resources or activities to enhance the likelihood of progress toward the objectives — or they can consider changing the objectives. (Rather than holding a program manager accountable for achieving progress toward a crime-reduction objective that appeared to be unrealistic, for example, higher-level managers might agree to hold the manager accountable for establishing a system for documenting the extent to which a specific approach reduces crime.)

## Unavailability of Relevant Information
## on Program Performance

When managers and policymakers have not agreed on a set of program objectives in terms of which the program will be managed and held accountable, evaluators' attempts to measure program performance are often frustratingly unsuccessful. Needed program performance data often prove to be unobtainable or too costly to collect; needed comparison data are even less likely to be available.

Evaluability assessment helps those in charge of a program to get the input needed to achieve agreement on appropriate program objectives and program performance indicators; to develop appropriate program performance measures; and to gain the cooperation and support needed to ensure the availability of valid, reliable data on program performance.

## Management Inability or Unwillingness to Act

Program managers and policymakers act on the basis of their entire past lives, most of which have been lived successfully without systematic information on program results. Program managers and policymakers are, therefore, often unwilling to absorb and use evaluation results. Some program managers lack the authority to take actions needed to improve program performance. In such cases, it may be necessary to involve higher-level managers and policymakers.

Evaluability assessment involves many management and policy levels in decisions on program objectives and information priorities. It helps those in charge to decide on intended uses of program performance information when the decisions are being made to collect the information. Evaluability assessment thus reduces the likelihood of that all-too-familiar evaluation phenomenon "information in search of a user." Early and continuing involvement of the managers and policymakers tends to facilitate the use of evaluation findings.[2] Agreement on intended uses of information also tends to facilitate use of evaluation findings.[3]

## Management Inability to Communicate the Value of Program Activities

Especially around budget time, many government and nonprofit organizations face difficulties in communicating what their activities are accomplishing. Available data demonstrate that staff are employed and that money is being spent, but convincing evidence of organizational effectiveness either is lacking or is embedded in case studies that are too voluminous for easy communication.[4] Evaluability assessment helps those in charge of public and nonprofit organizations to agree on outcome-oriented objectives and performance indicators that will facilitate efficient documentation and communication of organizational accomplishments.

## ORIGIN AND EVOLUTION OF EVALUABILITY ASSESSMENT

Evaluability assessment originated in the Urban Institute's program evaluation research group, as a result of the group's efforts to identify and solve problems inhibiting useful evaluation; in particular, problems inhibiting management use of evaluation to improve program performance. Reflecting on the results of past evaluations, the Urban Institute evaluation group concluded that evaluation is unlikely to result in program improvement unless three conditions are satisfied:

— *Program objectives, important side effects, and priority information needs are well defined* (that is, program managers have agreed on a set of measurable objectives and program performance indicators in terms of which the program is to be assessed and managed).

— *Program objectives are plausible* (that is, there is some likelihood that the objectives will be achieved).
— *Intended uses of information are well defined* (that is, program managers have agreed on intended uses of program performance information).

The "evaluability" (or "manageability") conditions have been stated in slightly different ways in different publications.[5] In this book, I try to simplify the statements of the conditions and of the method itself, to enhance the usefulness of the evaluability assessment approach.

Evaluability assessment developed in three stages, which correspond to the steps taken in conducting evaluability assessment as we now understand it: (1) clarifying program intent (1973-1975); (2) exploring program reality (1974-1977); and (3) assisting policy, management, and evaluation decisions (1978-present).

Evaluability assessment originally focused on the need for agreement on the objectives and performance indicators in terms of which program performance would be assessed. The initial focus was on understanding the decision environment; identifying relevant managers and policymakers; documenting the expectations, assumptions, and priorities of program managers, policymakers, and relevant interest groups; bounding the program to be evaluated; and identifying the performance indicators (types of evidence) in terms of which the program would be assessed and held accountable.

Evaluability assessment soon added a strong emphasis on getting evaluators into close contact with program reality before final decisions were made on program objectives and performance measurements. This second focus was on understanding program operations; estimating the likelihood that program objectives would be achieved; and clarifying the feasibility and cost of measuring program inputs, program activities, and program outcomes.

When examined in terms of the three evaluability criteria (agreed-on program objectives and performance indicators, plausible objectives, agreed-on uses of information), many programs appear poorly designed — not ready to be managed for results and not ready for evaluation work aimed at documenting and improving performance and results. Rather than labeling such programs as unmanageable or unevaluable, evaluators added a third evaluability assessment focus: helping those in charge to change the program to enhance the likelihood of results-oriented management and useful program evaluation. Here the evaluators identified — and helped managers to choose from among — program change options, each of which specified a set of plausible program objectives, a set of agreed-on program performance indicators, and one or more intended uses of each type of data to be collected.

Over the years since 1977, evaluability assessment has been implemented on a broad scale, included in standards and policies for conduct of program evaluation, modified, and improved. During this period evaluability assessment has come to be seen not as a rigid set of procedural steps but as a spirit and method directed at results-oriented management and management-oriented evaluation. In this phase, evaluability assessment has emerged as a member of a family of relatively inexpensive evaluation processes that managers and policymakers can use to set plausible, measurable program objectives; to identify changes in program activities that will contribute to improved program performance; and to identify evaluations, monitoring systems, and information systems that will contribute to demonstrably effective program performance.

Evaluability assessment has been incorporated into the policies and activities of the U.S. Department of Health and Human Services, the U.S. Department of Education, the Auditor General and the Comptroller General of Canada, the Evaluation Research Society of America, and many other organizations. In many instances, evaluability assessment occurs not as a separate activity but as the initial step in a larger evaluation.

## THE EVALUABILITY ASSESSMENT PROCESS

In this section we discuss the evaluability assessment process in more detail, presenting a simple example of the use of evaluability assessment in clarifying program objectives and in identifying options for program evaluation and for program improvement.

## Clarifying Program Intent, Side Effects of Interest, and Priority Information Needs

The initial focus of evaluability assessment was — and is — on establishing agreement on management and policy information needs. Here the evaluator documents program objectives, expectations, causal assumptions, information needs, and priorities of relevant managers, policymakers, and interest groups, clarifying the performance indicators (types of evidence) in terms of which the program will be assessed and managed.

Believing that evaluators often attempt to serve too many audiences (and therefore serve none well), Pamela Horst and her colleagues suggested that evaluators first identify those managers and policymakers who have the most influence on relevant program and policy decisions and then document the program design from their points of view.[6]

Here the evaluators use three sources of information: (1) program documentation (the program's authorizing legislation; legislative history; program regulations, guidelines, and annual reports; budget justifications; research, evaluation, and audit reports; speeches; organization charts; grant applications; and the like); (2) interviews with small numbers of program managers and policymakers in the executive and legislative branches of government; and (3) interviews with representatives of small numbers of relevant interest groups. On the basis of information from these sources, the evaluators develop two sets of products that promote fruitful dialogue between managers and evaluators. These products (program design models and lists of currently agreed-on program performance indicators) document the extent of agreement on program objectives among policymakers, managers, and interest groups, and document the types of information that could be developed in terms of agreed-on objectives and performance indicators.

### Program Design Models

*Program design models* (or *logic models*) present the program design (the resources allocated to the program, intended program activities, expected program outcomes, and assumed causal linkages) from the points of view of managers, policymakers, or key interest groups. An important part of the development of program design models is identification of intermediate outcome objectives that lead from program activities to intended program impacts.

In a typical technical assistance program, for example, program documentation and interviews with program managers and policymakers reveal agreement on a program design like that presented in Figure 2-1. (Technical assistance programs are typical of a large class of information programs intended to influence the behavior of organizations. The "technical assistance" may, in any given instance, be program regulations, guidelines, manuals, or inservice training.)

Program design models like Figure 2-1 present the key events in the intended program and the assumed causal connections among those events. With the agreed-on program performance indicators to be discussed next, program design models focus attention on management-oriented evaluations that might be relevant: Occurrence of the expected results could be tracked in a program monitoring system or management information system; the assumed causal connections could be tested in one or more evaluations.

In evaluability assessment, evaluators do not hypothesize the program design. Instead, evaluators extract the program design (in particular, the events expected to lead from program activities to intended impacts) from the key actors in and around the program — and ensure that the program design is acceptable to key program managers before a full-scale evaluation is undertaken. Management's program design, which may evolve during the course of an evaluability assessment, is the framework for decisions on the collection and analysis of program performance data.

In many programs, managers and policymakers agree on the intended program in all important respects. In other programs, however, there will be conflicts among managers and policymakers over the program objectives. As long as some of those in charge of the program are interested in a particular objective, the objective is likely to be included in program management's (revised) program design and in subsequent program monitoring or evaluation.

*Agreed-on Program Performance Indicators*

In most programs, management has a system for monitoring program activities but has not clearly defined the intended outcomes

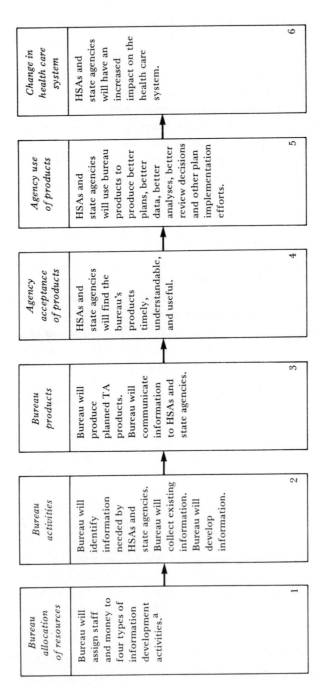

| Bureau allocation of resources | Bureau activities | Bureau products | Agency acceptance of products | Agency use of products | Change in health care system |
|---|---|---|---|---|---|
| Bureau will assign staff and money to four types of information development activities.[a] | Bureau will identify information needed by HSAs and state agencies. Bureau will collect existing information. Bureau will develop information. | Bureau will produce planned TA products. Bureau will communicate information to HSAs and state agencies. | HSAs and state agencies will find the bureau's products timely, understandable, and useful. | HSAs and state agencies will use bureau products to produce better plans, better data, better analyses, better review decisions and other plan implementation efforts. | HSAs and state agencies will have an increased impact on the health care system. |
| 1 | 2 | 3 | 4 | 5 | 6 |

[a] Assess HSA and State Agency needs, collect existing information, produce and develop new information, disseminate information to health planners in HSAs and State Agencies.

**Figure 2-1 Program III: Developing and Disseminating Discretionary Technical Assistance Products (Program Logic from Bureau's Perspective)** (*Source:* Joseph S. Wholey and others, *Evaluability Assessment for the Bureau of Health Planning and Resources Development, DHEW: Bureau Program III: Developing and Disseminating Discretionary Technical Assistance Products* (Washington, D.C.: The Urban Institute, 1977), p. 6.

and intended impacts of program activities. In a typical technical assistance program, for example, program documentation and interviews with program managers reveal agreement on performance indicators for the first four events in the program design (see Table 2-1). Technical assistance program managers typically monitor program activities by comparing actual program activities with those specified in some type of management-by-objectives (MBO) system, and monitor products produced and disseminated by comparing draft and final products with those scheduled to be

**Table 2-1   Technical Assistance Program: Management's Agreed-on Program Performance Indicators**

| Events | Agreed-on performance indicators | Data sources |
|---|---|---|
| 1. Resources are allocated and expended | 1a. Staff years allocated | 1a. Budget |
| | 1b. Staff years expended | 1b. Work measurement system |
| | 1c. Contract funds allocated | 1c. Budget |
| | 1d. Contract funds expended | 1d. Accounting system |
| 2. Staff and contractor activities | 2a. Planned vs. actual schedule of staff and contractor activities | 2a. Program records |
| 3. Products are produced and disseminated | 3a. Product produced: draft, final | 3a. Program records |
| | 3b. Product disseminated | 3b. Program records |
| 4. Products are accepted by local agencies | 4a. Product was considered useful by local agencies | 4a. —— |
| 5. Products are used by local agencies | 5a. —— | 5a. —— |
| 6. Changes occur in health care system | 6a. —— | 6a. —— |

*Source:* Adapted from Joseph S. Wholey and others, *Evaluability Assessment for the Bureau of Health Planning and Resources Development, DHEW: Bureau Program III: Developing and Disseminating Discretionary Technical Assistance Products* (Washington, D.C.: The Urban Institute, 1977), pp. 10 and 32.

produced and disseminated. Managers of technical assistance programs usually do not get systematic data on the extent of their success in meeting the program's outcome and impact objectives, however. Instead, they rely on informal, unsystematic feedback to get clues as to the program's effectiveness.

## Exploring Program Reality

The second focus of evaluability assessment is on program reality. Here the evaluator documents the feasibility of measuring program performance and estimates the likelihood that program objectives will be achieved. Believing that evaluators too often attempt measurements and comparisons that later prove to be infeasible or too costly, Joe Nay and his colleagues recommended that, as a step toward the design of evaluations or information systems, evaluators spend some time documenting the program activities actually under way.[7] By documenting flows of resources, flows of clients (or other entities of interest), and flows of program performance information, evaluators learn what program performance information could be developed in a full-scale evaluation or management system; and they can estimate the likelihood that program objectives will be achieved. Examination of program operations may reveal that program reality is far from the program design envisioned by those at higher management and policy levels.

Using existing documentation (program data systems, project reports, monitoring reports, research reports, evaluation reports, audit reports) and site visits to a small number of projects, the evaluators determine the extent to which intended resources, activities, and outcomes are likely to materialize. At this point, three intermediate products may be developed: models of resource flows, process flow, and information flows. These products, which usually are not presented to management as such, provide information that the evaluators can use in developing and defending their findings.

### Resource Flows

By making rough estimates of the flows of resources to program activities (on the basis of budget documents, contracts, MBO systems, or work measurement systems, for example), the evaluator begins to move from program rhetoric to identification of the priority objectives in which appreciable resources are being invested. In the Bureau of Health Planning and Resources Development technical assistance program, for example, it turned out that few resources were going into determining what problems existed at local level or determining what solutions work at local level (see Figure 2-2).

*Process Flow*

In a typical technical assistance program, program documentation, interviews with those who operate the program, and interviews with those served by the program reveal a flow of technical assistance products among "states," like those illustrated in Figure

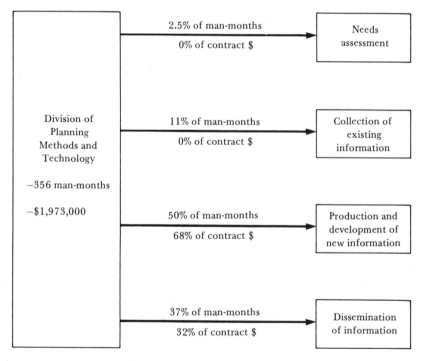

**Figure 2-2  Technical Assistance Program: Resource Flows** (*Source:* Joseph S. Wholey and others, *Evaluability Assessment for the Bureau of Health Planning and Resources Development, DHEW: Bureau Program III: Developing and Disseminating Discretionary Technical Assistance Products* (Washington, D.C.: The Urban Institute, 1977), p. 22.)

2-3. Process flow models like Figure 2-3 present the states in which an entity of interest can be, and the flows of that entity among states. The process flow model displays the points at which program performance measurements could be taken.

## Information Flows

In a typical technical assistance program, the evaluators' exploration of program reality reveals systematic information flows like those displayed in Figure 2-4:

— Management systematically collects information on products produced and disseminated.
— That information is used by management to control staff and contractor activities.
— Information is not systematically collected on whether the technical assistance products are accepted and used by local agencies, or whether use of the products results in expected changes in the environment.

## Plausibility Analyses

To assist decisions on the set of objectives in terms of which a program is to be managed and held accountable, my colleagues and I added an analysis of the plausibility of program objectives.[8] Based on what has been learned from program documentation, from interviews with program managers, policymakers, and representatives of relevant interest groups, and from site visits, the evaluators estimate the likelihood that each objective will be achieved at an acceptable level of accomplishment. These plausibility analyses have changed evaluability assessment from a pre-evaluation process to an evaluation process.

In many technical assistance programs, for example, exploration of program reality reveals that there are serious problems in getting products produced and disseminated — and even more serious problems in getting those products accepted and used. The summary presentation in Figure 2-5 conveys these judgments succinctly.

The plausibility analysis represents the evaluator's judgments on the likely success of the program — judgments based on available

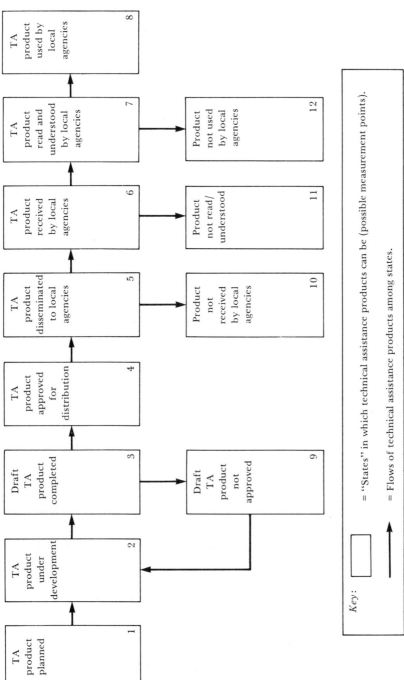

**Figure 2-3  Technical Assistance Program: Process Flow**

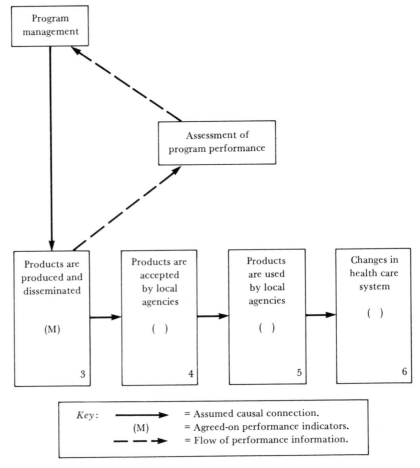

**Figure 2-4  Technical Assistance Program: Current Information Flows**

information and subject to later revision. Even on the basis of a small amount of information, it is often possible to conclude that success is unlikely or is highly uncertain. When such judgments are presented to managers or policymakers with supporting evidence, those in charge can use the information in decisions on possible changes in program design or information system design.

## Assisting Policy and Management Decisions

The first focus of evaluability assessment was on program intent; the second, on program reality. The third focus is on management

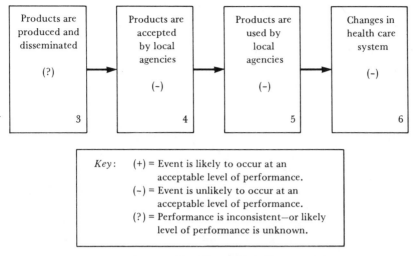

Figure 2-5   Technical Assistance Program: Plausibility of Program Objectives

use of evaluability assessment information to improve program design, program performance, and use of program performance information. Using the information gathered and analyzed in the first two evaluability assessment steps, the evaluators are now in position to work with management, clarifying the implications of what has been learned and exploring options for program change and program improvement.

## The Evaluable Program (Status Quo Option)

One option is always the *status quo* option, which would leave the program as it currently exists. The *evaluable model* of the program presents, in summary form, an evaluation of the program design in terms of three evaluability criteria. The *evaluable program* is that portion of the program which is currently manageable in terms of a set of realistic program objectives and agreed-on program performance indicators. For our technical assistance program, for example, the evaluable program would include only the first three events in the program design: allocation of resources to technical assistance, staff and contractor activities, and production and dissemination of technical assistance products. Objectives 4, 5, and 6 would be missing from the evaluable model because objectives 4, 5, and 6 are unrealistic and because agreed-on performance indicators have not been identified for objectives 5 and 6.

*Policy, Management, and Information Options*

The evaluability assessment is typically a powerful critique of the program design. In terms of the three evaluability criteria, few government programs look good, at least initially. The evaluators now help management to explore possible changes in the program design that could improve the likelihood of demonstrably effective performance.

Believing that the collection of program performance information should always be related to an intended use of the information, and believing that priority should be given to collection of information likely to improve program management and program performance, Richard Schmidt and his colleagues worked with key managers and policymakers to explore program change options implied by the evaluability assessment findings.[9] Three types of program design options were developed and explored:

1. options for changes in program resources or objectives (now called "policy options")
2. options for changes in program activities ("management options")
3. options for changes in collection and use of program performance information ("information options").

Working with management, evaluators explore the implications of the status quo and other program design options, gathering and presenting new data if necessary to facilitate management decisions on program resources, program activities, program objectives, or collection and use of program performance information.

Results-oriented technical assistance program managers would probably find the status quo unacceptable. Results-oriented managers would probably want to achieve and demonstrate progress toward outcome or impact objectives; for example, objectives 4 and 5: local agency acceptance and use of technical assistance products. Deciding to hold the program accountable on such outcome objectives would be a "policy" choice that would in turn imply selection of both information and management options.

Table 2-2 presents information options for technical assistance programs: performance measures that results-oriented managers might use to assess and manage a technical assistance program.

Table 2–2 Technical Assistance Program: Possible New Performance Indicators

| Events | Possible new performance indicators | Data sources |
|---|---|---|
| 4. Products are accepted by local agencies | 4a. Product was received by potential user | 4a. Telephone surveys |
| | 4b. Product was read and understood by potential user | 4b. Telephone surveys |
| | 4c. Product was considered useful by local agency | 4c. Telephone surveys |
| | 4d. Product presented significant knowledge or capability that potential user did not already have | 4d. Telephone surveys |
| 5. Products are used by local agencies | 5a. Decision was made to use product in local agency operations | 5a. User documentation |
| | 5b. Effort was made to use product in local agency operations | 5b. User documentation |
| | 5c. Product was successfully used in local agency operations | 5c. User documentation |
| 6. Changes occur in health care system | 6a. Use of product led to expected results | 6a. User documentation |

Source: Adapted from Joseph S. Wholey and others, *Evaluability Assessment for the Bureau of Health Planning and Resources Development, DHEW: Bureau Program III: Developing and Disseminating Technical Assistance Products* (Washington, D.C.: The Urban Institute, 1977), p. 32.

Here the evaluators suggest a set of possible performance indicators that appear relevant to policy and management information needs and could be translated into feasible program performance measures. Table 2–3 illustrates the types of program outcome data that results-oriented managers might use in managing a technical assistance program .

Management selection of any or all of the performance indicators in Table 2–2 would represent management's intent to assess and manage the technical assistance program in terms of the types of outcome and impact objectives often cited in legislative/budget justifications. Selection of one or more of these new performance

Table 2-3  Technical Assistance Program: Hypothetical New Performance Data

|  | Product No. 1 | Product No. 5 |
|---|---|---|
| *Number of appropriate local agency staff surveyed* | 100[a] | 200[b] |
| 4a. Product was received by potential user | 90% | 40% |
| 4b. Product was read and understood by potential user | 70 | 30 |
| 4c. Product was considered useful by local agency | 60 | 10 |
| 4d. Product presented significant knowledge or capability that potential user did not already have | 50 | 10 |
| 5a. Decision was made to use product in local agency operations | 40 | 5 |
| 5b. Effort was made to use product in local agency operations | 40 | 5 |
| 5c. Product was successfully used in local agency operations | 20 | 2 |

[a]Sample survey responses are subject to random error of approximately 10 percentage points.
[b]Sample survey responses are subject to random error of approximately 7 percentage points.

*Source:* Adapted from Joseph S. Wholey and others, *Evaluability Assessment for the Bureau of Health Planning and Resources Development, DHEW: Bureau Program III: Developing and Disseminating Discretionary Technical Assistance Products* (Washington, D.C.: The Urban Institute, 1977), pp. 34-35.

measures would not, however, do much to improve program results.

Results-oriented technical assistance program managers might wish to change the program by adding new activities designed to enhance the likelihood of progress toward the program's outcome and impact objectives. Possible new program activities of this kind (for example, documentation of best local practices as bases for development of useful technical assistance products) would now be presented as "management options."

The evaluators present evaluability assessment findings and program design options to managers and key staff in a series of memoranda, individual briefings, and decision-making meetings. An initial meeting might cover program design models and agreed-on program performance indicators (Figure 2-1 and Table 2-1); a second meeting, the plausibility of program objectives (Figure 2-5) and the feasibility of relevant measurements and comparisons; a third meeting, the implications of the status quo option and a number of options for changing the program design to enhance the likelihood of effective program performance or to better document program accomplishments.

The evaluability assessment proceeds by successive iterations, with the initial specification of program design models, agreed-on performance measures, and program options all subject to revision on the basis of additional information.

## CONCLUSION

To meet public needs and rebuild public confidence in government, government managers must achieve demonstrable improvements in the performance and results of the programs for which they are responsible. Though improved government performance will not in itself restore public confidence in government, it is a necessary step in the process.

Evaluability assessments help managers to establish realistic, outcome-oriented program objectives by bringing together information on the expectations, priorities, and information needs of policymakers, managers, and relevant interest groups; and by providing informed estimates of the likelihood that various objectives will be achieved. Evaluability assessments help build a consensus on program objectives and priorities that is stable enough to outlast changes in individual managers or policymakers. Evaluability assessments focus managers' attention, in particular, on "intermediate outcome objectives" (outcome objectives that lead from program activities to intended program impacts), thereby facilitating a shift from process-oriented management to results-oriented management.

Evaluability assessments also facilitate needed changes in program activities by identifying program objectives whose accomplishment is unrealistic or uncertain — and by pointing out opportunities to improve program performance while there is still time.

Over the years since 1977, evaluability assessment has been tested, refined, and extensively used. In the U.S. Department of Health and Human Services between 1978 and 1980, for example, evaluability assessments of more than twenty programs resulted in changes in program design or changes in collection/use of program performance information in most of the programs assessed. In Chapter 3, we present examples of management use of evaluability assessment in setting realistic, measurable objectives for their programs. In Chapter 4, we present managers' reactions on the usefulness of the evaluability assessment approach.

## NOTES TO CHAPTER 2

1. An earlier version of this chapter was presented at the Symposium on Program Evaluation: A Tool for Health Care Administrators, Hofstra University, Hempstead, N.Y., July 16, 1981, and will appear in Bernard Rosen and William Schmelter, eds., *Program Evaluation and the Delivery of Health Care* (Springfield, Ill.: Charles C. Thomas, forthcoming).

2. See John D. Waller and others, *Developing Useful Evaluation Capability: Lessons from the Model Evaluation Program,* Report prepared for the National Institute of Law Enforcement and Criminal Justice (Washington, D.C.: The Urban Institute, 1978).

3. See, for example, Murray Levine, *From State Hospital to Psychiatric Center* (Lexington, Mass.: D. C. Heath and Company, 1980), pp. 61-73; and Joseph S. Wholey, "Using Evaluation to Improve Program Performance," in Robert A. Levine and others, eds., *Evaluation Research and Practice: Comparative and International Perspectives* (Beverly Hills, Calif.: Sage Publications, 1981), pp. 92-106, and in Howard E. Freeman and Marian A. Solomon, eds., *Evaluation Studies Review Annual,* vol. 6 (Beverly Hills, Calif.: Sage Publications, 1981), pp. 55-69.

4. John Scanlon has noted the problems managers face in communicating voluminous qualitative information to higher policy levels. John W. Scanlon, "Developing Performance Measures" (Lecture at the University of Southern California's Washington Public Affairs Center, Washington, D.C., November 23, 1980).

5. See Pamela Horst and others, "Program Management and the Federal Evaluator," *Public Administration Review,* July/August 1974, pp. 300-308; Joseph S. Wholey and others, "If You Don't Care Where You Get To, Then It

Doesn't Matter Which Way You Go," in Gene M. Lyons, ed., *Social Research and Public Policies: The Dartmouth/OECD Conference* (Hanover, N.H.: Dartmouth College, 1975); Joseph S. Wholey and others, "Evaluation: When Is It Really Needed?" *Evaluation*, vol. 2, no. 2 (1975), pp. 89–93; John W. Scanlon and others, "Evaluability Assessment: Avoiding Types III and IV Errors," in G. Ronald Gilbert and Patrick J. Conklin, *Evaluation Management: A Selection of Readings* (Charlottesville, Va.: U.S. Office of Personnel Management, Federal Executive Institute, FEI B-12, 1979), pp. 43–59; and Richard E. Schmidt, John W. Scanlon, and James B. Bell, *Evaluability Assessment: Making Public Programs Work Better* (Rockville, Md.: U.S. Department of Health, Education, and Welfare, Project Share, Human Services Monograph No. 14, 1979).

6. Horst and others, "Program Management and the Federal Evaluator."

7. Joe N. Nay and others, *The National Institute's Information Machine: A Case Study of the National Evaluation Program*, Report prepared for the National Institute of Law Enforcement and Criminal Justice (Washington, D.C.: The Urban Institute, 1977); and Comptroller General of the United States, *Finding Out How Programs Are Working: Some Suggestions for Congressional Oversight* (Washington, D.C.: U.S. General Accounting Office, 1977).

8. Joseph S. Wholey and others, *Evaluability Assessment for the Bureau of Health Planning and Resources Development, DHEW*, 5 vols., Report prepared for the Department of Health, Education, and Welfare (Washington, D.C.: The Urban Institute, 1977).

9. Richard E. Schmidt and others, *Appalachian Regional Commission Health and Child Development Program*, Reports prepared for the Appalachian Regional Commission, Washington, D.C.: The Urban Institute, 1976). Also see Comptroller General, *Finding Out How Programs Are Working;* John W. Scanlon and John D. Waller, "Program Evaluation and Better Federal Programs" (Paper presented at the Annual Conference of the American Society for Public Administration, Phoenix, Ariz., 1978); John W. Scanlon and others, "Evaluability Assessment: Avoiding Types III and IV Errors," in G. Ronald Gilbert and Patrick J. Conklin, eds., *Evaluation Management: A Selection of Readings* (Charlottesville, Va.: U.S. Office of Personnel Management, Federal Executive Institute, FEI B-12, 1979), pp. 43–45; and Joseph S. Wholey and others, *Evaluability Assessment for the Bureau of Health Planning and Resources Development.*

# 3

## Setting Realistic,
## Measurable Objectives:
## Examples of
## the Evaluability
## Assessment Approach

### INTRODUCTION

Building on the preceding chapter, in this chapter we present three examples of the use of evaluability assessment in setting realistic, measurable program objectives; we examine issues and problems that arise in doing evaluability assessments; and we outline solutions that have emerged as the use of evaluability assessment has spread.[1] The examples, which are drawn from experiences in the U.S. Department of Health and Human Services and the Tennessee Department of Public Health, show how evaluators can assist federal and state policymakers and program managers in clarifying program expectations, in assessing the likelihood of effective program performance, in clarifying the feasibility of measuring program performance, and in helping managers and policymakers to improve program design and program performance. The examples are presented to give readers a working knowledge of the evaluability assessment process and products. Many other examples are becoming available as the evaluability assessment approach spreads in this country and in Canada.[2]

### EXAMPLE 1: CIVIL SERVICE REFORM

This section illustrates the use of evaluability assessment in setting clear, realistic objectives for civil service reform (in particular, for implementation of the Senior Executive Service in the U.S. Department of Health and Human Services) — and in identifying actions that would contribute to improved performance in the civil service reform program. Here the "program" was a major reform of the federal personnel system. The evaluability assessment and subsequent evaluation work focused, in particular, on the impact of the personnel system reform on executive management and on agency and program performance.[3]

The goals of the Civil Service Reform Act of 1978, P.L. 95-454, were to provide a competent, honest, and productive work force; to improve the quality of public service; and to improve the efficiency, effectiveness, and responsiveness of the government to national needs.[4] Among the means to these ends were the establishment of a Senior Executive Service (SES) of top-level federal executives, establishment of a new system of performance appraisal for senior executives and middle managers, and provisions for cash bonuses for senior executives and merit pay for middle managers. Civil service reform was directed at improvements in government management and improvements in the efficiency, effectiveness, and responsiveness of federal agencies and programs. Implementation of the Civil Service Reform Act provided federal agencies with an unusual opportunity to stimulate demonstrable improvements in the management and performance of federal programs.

In August 1979 the U.S. Office of Personnel Management asked the Department of Health and Human Services (HHS) to conduct an evaluation of the impact of civil service reform, in particular the impact of the Senior Executive Service. The Assistant Secretary for Personnel Administration asked the Assistant Secretary for Planning and Evaluation to conduct the evaluation, which was to focus, in particular, on (1) the planned and actual progress of HHS managers in defining and achieving improved program performance, and (2) the extent to which SES bonuses, program managers' merit pay, and cash awards reflect the definition and accomplishment of agreed-on, results-oriented program objectives.

Between September 1979 and August 1980, an evaluation team from the Office of the Assistant Secretary for Planning and Evaluation (ASPE) and an ASPE contractor (Consad Research Corporation) conducted an evaluability assessment of the Department's

Senior Executive Service "program." The evaluability assessment was designed to document the program objectives and expectations of SES program managers, policymakers, and SES members; to assess the likelihood that measurable progress would be made toward the Department's SES program objectives; to document intended uses of information on SES program performance; and to identify changes in program activities or uses of information through which program managers and policymakers could produce a better-designed, more effective SES program.[5]

### Documenting Program Intent

The evaluators reviewed the Civil Service Reform Act, its legislative history, and related literature on the Senior Executive Service. They then interviewed approximately twenty-five key policy staff in the U.S. Office of Management and Budget, in the Office of Personnel Management, and in the General Accounting Office, on House and Senate committee staffs, and in the Office of the Assistant Secretary for Personnel Administration. A consistent model of the intended SES program emerged from the evaluators' analysis of the program's legislative intent and from the interviews with key policymakers. This model was agreed to by the Assistant Secretary for Personnel Administration, with very minor modifications (see Figure 3-1).

### Assessing the Likelihood of
### Effective Program Performance

The evaluation team then interviewed approximately thirty HHS members of the new Senior Executive Service. Most of these senior executives agreed that the evaluation team had captured the intent of the SES program. Many were concerned about implementation issues, however, and had reactions like these:

— "If I know that so-and-so got a bonus and I didn't, I'll be angry."
— "We were pressured to join the SES before we had any idea how the system would work."
— "Performance appraisal plans are meaningless."[6]

Based on findings from the earlier stages of the study, the evaluation team examined the expected events and the assumed causal

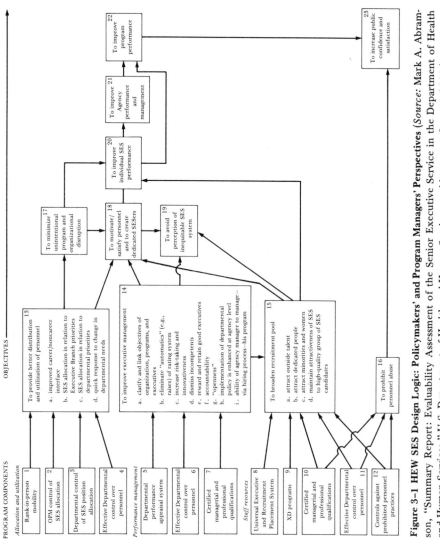

**Figure 3-1 HEW SES Design Logic: Policymakers' and Program Managers' Perspectives** (*Source:* Mark A. Abramson, "Summary Report: Evaluability Assessment of the Senior Executive Service in the Department of Health and Human Services," U.S. Department of Health and Human Services working paper, January 1981.)

linkages in the SES program design, responding to two questions:

— Was there anything in the literature or the study team's own experience that suggested that the design or some part of the SES program design was faulty or theoretically improbable?
— Was there any evidence that key events in the program design were not occurring or would not occur in the future?[7]

The evaluation team concluded that the SES program was conceptually sound, but identified five major problems in the program design:

*Problem 1: Lags in Public Perception of Government Executive Performance.* The program design assumed that, if HHS programs improved (Figure 3-1, Event 22), then the public's confidence in government would increase (Event 23). The evaluation team noted, however, that public confidence in government might well be almost independent of the performance of government agencies and programs.

*Problem 2: Lack of Departmental Policy Regarding Links Between Individual Performance Plans and Agency and Program Performance.* The program design assumed the existence of causal linkages among individual performance, agency performance, and program performance (Figure 3-1, Events 20, 21, and 22). Based on the interviews and the guidance material on SES performance plans, however, the evaluation team concluded that these assumed causal links were problematic. The team expected that many individual performance plans would ignore agency and program objectives, that those who tried to include them in performance plans would have difficulties, and that those agency and program objectives included in individual performance plans would fall short of policymakers' desires.

*Problem 3: Absence of Supportive Attitudes Within the SES.* Many of the senior executives interviewed exhibited a great deal of cynicism about the new personnel system. Furthermore, the literature suggested that the planned performance planning and performance appraisal systems might not work.

*Problem 4: Difficulty of Detecting Prohibited Political Personnel Abuse.* Some senior executives expressed concern that performance appraisal systems might be set up in such ways as to cause individuals to fail — and that such abuses might be difficult to detect through any routine monitoring system.

*Problem 5:    Equal Rewards for Unequal Performance.* To avoid perceptions of inequity in SES bonus awards, it appeared that the Department would have to develop some system for scaling bonuses based on "degree of job difficulty."

*Summary*

Given the five problems just identified, the evaluation team concluded that four sets of SES program objectives (Events 16, 18-19, 20-22, and 23) were unlikely to be achieved unless changes were made in the SES program.[8]

## Deciding on Program Objectives and Evaluation Strategy

Next, a series of policy and management options were developed for consideration by the Assistant Secretary for Personnel Administration.[9]

### 1. Public Confidence

With regard to objective 23, "to increase public confidence and satisfaction," for example, the options paper discussed four options open to the Department:

- (Option 1.1) HHS gives up objective 23, "to increase public confidence and satisfaction."
- (Option 1.2) HHS formally recommends that another government unit (the General Accounting Office or the Office of Personnel Management) assume responsibility for this objective.
- (Option 1.3) HHS decides to achieve measurable progress toward this objective. HHS develops specific programmatic activities to achieve this objective.
- (Option 1.4) For selected programs, the Secretary directs that increasing public confidence be made a major objective for program managers.

Based on the evaluation team's analysis of the options, the Assistant Secretary decided that he would not take responsibility for demonstrating progress toward the objective of increasing public confidence in government.

## 2. Linking Individual and Agency and Program Objectives

With regard to objectives 21 and 22 ("to improve agency performance and management; to improve program performance"), the options paper discussed five options open to the Department:

— (Option 2.1) Put in place a system to ensure that, for all 120 HHS programs, linkages exist between individual objectives and program objectives (that is, all performance plans must either incorporate program objectives or specify job relationships to program objectives).
— (Option 2.2a) Put in place a system to ensure linkages necessary to connect individual plans and the forty programs in the Secretary's management-by-objectives system.
— (Option 2.2b) Put in place a system to ensure linkages necessary to connect individual plans and the objectives for the twelve programs in a special HHS performance improvement initiative.
— (Option 2.2c) Test the approach in several agencies within the Department. All the programs within those agencies would be selected to implement the approach.
— (Option 2.3) The HHS Executive Management Resources Council would announce that subsequent nominations of senior executives for presidential "meritorious" or "distinguished" ranks would give great weight to the extent to which senior executives with line management experience had demonstrated high or improved program performance in terms of agreed-on, results-oriented program objectives and performance indicators.

In response to this general concern, the Secretary of Health and Human Services directed that all senior executives with significant responsibility for one of the objectives in the Secretary's management-by-objectives system must include those objectives in their performance plans.

## 3. Supportive Attitudes Among SES Members

In response to an analysis of options for solving the third problem, "absence of supportive attitudes within the SES," the Assistant Secretary decided to engage in a small set of activities designed to minimize negative attitudes among senior executives within the Department.

### 4. *Preventing Prohibited Personnel Abuse*

In response to an analysis of options for solving the fourth problem, "difficulty of detecting prohibited political personnel abuse," it was decided that the Assistant Secretary would conduct a limited number of educational activities in the area of prohibited personnel practices but that a major effort would not be launched in this area.

### 5. *Equal Rewards for Unequal Performance*

In response to a discussion of options for solving the fifth problem, the Office of the Assistant Secretary for Personnel Administration prepared a "degree of difficulty" adjustment process that could be used in determining the size of individual bonuses, and the HHS Executive Resources Management Council agreed to transmit these "degree of difficulty" differentiation guidelines to the Department's Executive Resource Boards.

### *Decisions on Evaluation Strategy*

Following these decisions on objectives and program activities, the evaluation team developed potential performance measures for each of the objectives in the SES program design. The performance indicators were reviewed by the Assistant Secretary for Personnel Administration and his staff, and the Assistant Secretary and his staff agreed on appropriate performance indicators for each objective in the SES program design. Based on these agreements, the evaluation team prepared a set of evaluation alternatives, and agreement was reached on the design for a full-scale evaluation of the impact of the SES program in the Department.[10]

The effect of these decisions was that the Assistant Secretary for Personnel Administration assumed responsibility for attempting to achieve measurable progress toward SES program objectives 1–22, but did not accept responsibility for attempting to achieve measurable progress toward objective 23.

## Conclusion

In June 1981 the Department of Health and Human Services began a three-year evaluation of the implementation and impact of civil service reform in the Department. This evaluation was a direct follow-on to the evaluability assessment. The evaluation contract required the contractor (1) to ascertain the attitudes and perspectives of HHS SES members toward SES through a series of questionnaires and interviews, and (2) to ascertain the impact, if any, of civil service reform and the Senior Executive Service on the management and performance of HHS programs.[11] Other parts of the evaluation were to be done in-house.

It is worth noting that, throughout this evaluability assessment, the evaluators prepared no reports. Instead, they transmitted evaluability assessment findings and options to the Assistant Secretary for Personnel Administration and his staff through a series of brief memoranda, option papers, briefings, and work sessions. A brief summary report was prepared after the evaluability assessment was completed, and was published as part of the request for proposals (RFP) for the full-scale evaluation.[12]

## EXAMPLE 2: COMMUNITY SUPPORT PROGRAM

This section illustrates the use of evaluability assessment in setting realistic, measurable objectives for a relatively hard-to-measure program — and in identifying actions that would contribute to demonstrably effective program performance. Here the program was a federally funded demonstration program.[13]

The Community Support Program was initiated by the National Institute of Mental Health (NIMH) in 1977 to encourage states to develop comprehensive, coordinated community-based care for the chronically mentally ill, including those returning to their communities from state mental hospitals. The objectives of the program were to meet the comprehensive needs of the chronically mentally ill in the community, not just to meet their mental health needs. Essential components of the Community Support Program (CSP) therefore included psychosocial rehabilitation, assistance in obtaining entitlements (for example, income support), assistance in improving employability, residential opportunities, and other supportive services. The fiscal year 1979 program included nineteen state projects, funded at $300,000 to $350,000 per year for three-year periods. Fiscal year 1979 appropriations totaled $7.6 million. The national program had a staff of twelve, including three staff members serving in the federal government under the Intergovernmental Personnel Act.

Between October 1979 and June 1980, a work group consisting of one staff member from the HEW Office of the Assistant Secretary for Planning and Evaluation (ASPE), two staff members from the NIMH Division of Biometry and Epidemiology (responsible for CSP evaluation), one staff member from the NIMH Division of Mental Health Service Programs, one staff member from the Community Support Program branch, one staff member from the Office of the Assistant Secretary for Health, and four staff members from an ASPE contractor (Macro Systems) conducted an evaluability assessment of the Community Support Program. The Community Support Program evaluability assessment was initiated at the request of the Division of Mental Health Service Programs, which was interested in using the assessment to make program design changes and to develop a realistic evaluation plan for the program.

## Documenting the Intended Community Support Program

Through review of CSP documentation and initial discussions with CSP staff, the work group defined the Community Support Program as a specific set of resources and activities of two sections of the NIMH Community Support and Rehabilitation Branch, in the Division of Mental Health Service Programs. CSP program design models (resources, activities, objectives, and causal linkages) were developed based on review of fifty-two documents, including the program's legislation and legislative history, reports of hearings before congressional committees, program guidelines, requests for proposals, contract files, project files, and several journal articles.[14]

The work group then interviewed three CSP managers, five other NIMH managers and policymakers, a congressional committee staff member, and representatives of six interest groups and professional groups, to document their expectations for the program, the problems they perceived in the program, and their information needs regarding the program (see Table 3–1). Though interviewees' priorities varied (for example, between service delivery and systems change goals), the interviews revealed broad agreement among CSP managers and policymakers regarding CSP program activities, objectives, and expectations. As seen by CSP program managers and policymakers, the Community Support Program was intended to achieve results of the kind presented in Figure 3–2. The congressional staff respondent and some interest groups also suggested that CSP projects should be responsible for influencing the mental health system to be more responsive to the needs of the chronically mentally ill.

For most of the objectives in the CSP program design, the evaluability assessment showed that performance indicators either did not exist or had not been agreed to.

## Documenting the Actual Community Support Program

The work group then reviewed available documentation on the nineteen CSP projects to get a clearer understanding of the range of activities under way. The first-year technical proposals and the first-year project reports were used to determine project characteristics and to classify projects.[15]

Based on review of the technical proposals and first-year reports, the work group selected a diverse group of projects for site visits. The CSP program manager then sent letters to each site selected, explaining the purpose of the planned visits.

Over a three-week period, two-person teams made field visits to four HEW regional offices and to ten CSP project sites (five state offices, and five local demonstration sites) to document CSP activities under way; to document the goals and objectives being sought at regional, state, and local levels; and to identify feasible measures of progress toward program goals (see Tables 3–2 and 3–3). In these site visits approximately eighty-five people were interviewed, and project records, reports, and other project materials were reviewed.

The site visits revealed that the actual program closely matched the intended program and that similar types of activities were under way at different sites. Common problems were identified,

**Table 3-1   CSP Program Manager and Policymaker Interview Guide**

1. What is your (or your Branch's/your Division's) relationship to CSP?
2. a. How is the CSP staffed and organized at the NIMH level?
   b. What components of NIMH are involved with the program, other than the CSP Branch?
   c. What agencies, external to NIMH, are involved with the CSP and how?
3. a. Can you describe the major activities of the CSP?
   b. What resources are applied to these activities?
4. How did the two types of contracts evolve?
5. How were the contractors selected?
6. From your perspective, what are the main purposes or objectives of the CSP? What is CSP trying to accomplish?
7. What accomplishments is the CSP likely to achieve in the next two or three years? What are your expectations?
8. How will the activities undertaken by/through the CSP produce these accomplishments? (Why would these activities produce those results?)
9. What kinds of information do you have on CSP performance?
   (If necessary, explore how contracts are monitored.)
10. How do you use this information?
11. a. What kinds of information do you (or CSP) need to assess program performance or accomplishments?
    b. How would this information be used?
12. What measure or indicators of program performance are relevant to the CSP?
13. a. What problems (conceptual or operational) face the CSP in meeting its objectives?
    b. How might these problems/difficulties be overcome?
14. What factors are likely to influence the program over the next two to five years?

*Source:* Beth Stroul and others, *Final Report of the Exploratory Evaluation of the National Institute of Mental Health Community Support Program* (Silver Spring, Md.: Macro Systems, 1980), Appendix B.

including scarcity of resources, problems in interagency collaboration, and definitional issues related to the target population and to community support system components.

Review of available program performance information showed that despite the collection of much narrative data, the available data were of questionable reliability, comparability, and usefulness. States mentioned burdensome reporting requirements as a

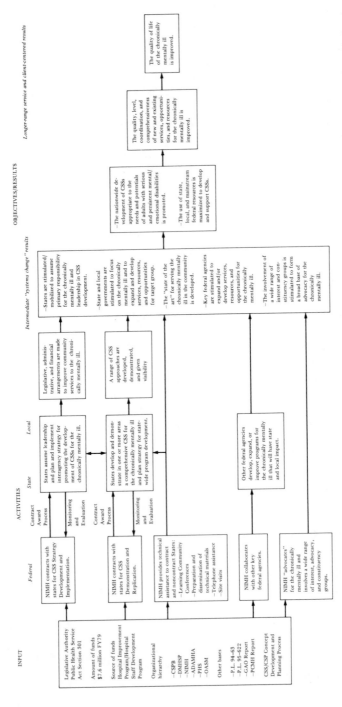

**Figure 3-2   Community Support Program Logic** (*Source:* Beth Stroul and others, *Final Report of the Exploratory Evaluation of the National Institute of Mental Health Community Support Program* (Silver Spring, Md.: Macro Systems, 1980), p. iv.)

**Table 3-2  CSP Field Visit Instructions**

The products of each field visit should include:

— Completed Interview Summary Forms for each interview.
— Complete list of written materials and documentation reviewed both on-site and in preparing for visit.
— A brief Field Visit Report compiling and summarizing all information for each site.
— Process flow models of each site.

What to look for on field visits:

— Descriptions of major project activities.
— Measurement indicators and statements of accomplishments and results.
— Data currently collected or potentially available.
— Project resources including amounts and sources of funding, staff, etc.

Also essential is information regarding:

— Relationships among key actors/agencies.
— Operating assumptions and approach.
— Problems/barriers.

What documents to review:

— Proposals ⎫
— Contracts ⎬  All relevant project materials at NIMH should be reviewed prior to visit.
— Reports ⎭

— Project descriptions ⎫
— Evaluation plans and reports ⎬  Should be reviewed on site.
— Other relevant records, documents, and materials ⎭

Who to interview:

*Regional office*(1-2 persons)
— Regional CSP Consultant/Coordinator.
— ADAMHA Division Commissioner.
*State office* (3-4 people)
— State level CSP Project Director.
— Key project personnel responsible for each major project activity (including data collection).
— Any other key persons knowledgeable about project.

**Table 3-2  Continued**

*Local demonstration site* (4–5 people)
— Local Program Director/Administrator.
— Key project personnel responsible for each major project activity
   (including data colection).
— Any other key persons knowledgeable about project.

Individual interviews with project staff should be conducted, rather than
group interviews.

*Source:* Adapted from Beth Stroul and others, *Final Report of the Exploratory Evaluation of the National Institute of Mental Health Community Support Program* (Silver
Spring, Md.: Macro Systems, 1980), Appendix E.

---

major problem; they also expressed needs for guidance and assistance in evaluation.

## Development and Refinement of Findings and Options

The work group then used the information collected to date
in performing (1) a qualitative assessment of the likelihood that
CSP program objectives would be achieved; (2) an assessment of
the extent of agreement on program performance indicators; and
(3) an assessment of the feasibility and usefulness of existing and
possible new program performance measures.[16]
   The evaluability assessment showed the following:

1. CSP resources were inadequate to achieve the program's broad
   range of objectives on a nationwide basis.
2. It was questionable whether CSP objectives at the local level
   could be achieved without significant federal support.
3. The efficiency of the interagency service coordination and
   collaboration approach was questionable.
4. The program lacked agreed-on performance measures and
   lacked information on program performance.
5. The planned new CSP grant mechanism should be structured
   to facilitate achievement of CSP objectives and to facilitate
   learning from the experience of CSP grantees.

   Next, the work group developed a large number of options for
solving the problems identified in the plausibility analysis.

Table 3-3  State and Local CSP Interview Guide

1. What is your role in the CSP project?
2. What are the main purposes or objectives of the project? What is it trying to accomplish?
3. What are the major activities of the project (mechanisms to achieve objectives)? (Probe for step-by-step descriptions of major operations or processes.)
4. How are you meeting the following contract requirements?

| Strategy | Demonstration |
| --- | --- |
| — Participatory planning process | — Implement the 10 CSS components in the local area |
| — Assessment of CSS needs and resources | |
| — Develop and implement CSS Action Plan | — Document/evaluate the "model" CSS |
| | — Statewide CSS development |

5. Why do you feel that your approach will achieve CSP objectives?
6. What are the resources available to the project?

   — Number of staff
   — Amount of funds (total annual budget)
   — Total cost as compared to federal share
   — List sources of funds

7. What evidence is necessary to see whether project objectives are met?
8. What data are currently collected (or potentially available)?
9. How is the information used? Does anything change based on the data?
10. What do you see as your project's major accomplishments or results to date?
11. How would you characterize or describe your interrelationships with CSP at other levels (Local, State, Regional Office, Federal) and with other key actors or agencies in your environment?
12. What problems or barriers do you face in achieving your objectives? What problems do you have with your contract? Other problems?
13. What would happen to your project without the Federal dollars? Could the project contine?
14. Where do you think your project will be in three to five years? What forces or factors will impact on your ability to operate effectively?

Source: Beth Stroul and others, Final Report of the Exploratory Evaluation of the Community Support Program (Silver Spring, Md.: Macro Systems, 1980), Appendix E.

## 1. Inadequate Resources for an Effective Nationwide Effort

With regard to the inadequacy of resources for an effective nation-wide program, the work group identified three options open to the program:

— (Option 1.1) Seek additional resources to expand CSP to a nationwide effort.
— (Option 1.2) Although management is reluctant to do so, the program description could be modified to reflect more modest goals.
— (Option 1.3) Hold CSP accountable for achieving its objectives only at demonstration and development sites.

## 2. Interagency Coordination and Collaboration

With regard to interagency coordination and collaboration, the work group identified three options for consideration by CSP management:

— (Option 3.1) Identify realistic leverage points (for example, legislation, financial incentives) to ensure the effectiveness of interagency activities; identify mechanisms to induce or provide conditions conducive to obtaining the cooperation of key agencies.
— (Option 3.2) Clarify the interagency collaboration process, including the responsibilities for such efforts at federal, state, and local levels, priority areas for interagency efforts, and so on.
— (Option 3.3) Identify alternative approaches to obtain requisite resources and services for the target population.

## 3. Lack of Agreed-on Performance Measures

With regard to the lack of agreed-on program performance indicators, the work group identified one option:

— (Option 4.1) Refine CSP performance indicators to develop a set of measures of program inputs, activities, and outcomes that are agreed upon by CSP managers and policymakers.

## Evaluability Assessment Results

At the request of CSP managers, two tasks were added to the evaluability assessment: (1) assistance in structuring the new CSP grant mechanism and program guidelines to maximize management's ability to shape the program toward achieving program objectives; (2) assistance in tailoring data collection and reporting requirements to agreed-on CSP objectives, performance indicators, and information needs.[17]

In the new CSP grant announcement and guidelines, the notion of "nationwide" development of community support systems (an unrealistic objective) was dropped; the nature and purpose of interagency collaboration were clarified; and the program's objectives with respect to the mental health system were clarified. Richard Woy, a member of the policy group for the CSP evaluation, notes that the resulting CSP grant announcement and guidelines thus provided a clearer picture of the intended Community Support Program and more coherent direction to grantees than would have been possible without the evaluability assessment.[18]

In addition, a follow-on effort was initiated to implement several of the options identified in the evaluability assessment, especially those related to operationalizing key CSP components and refining and testing appropriate program performance indicators. (The evaluability assessment had been paid for by the Office of the Assistant Secretary for Planning and Evaluation (ASPE); the costs of the follow-on effort were shared equally between ASPE and the National Institute of Mental Health.)

## A Note on the CSP Evaluability Assessment Process

The evaluability assessment process required the work group to work closely with CSP program managers throughout the evaluation. In addition, a policy group, consisting of program managers and policymakers from NIMH and ASPE, provided substantive input and guidance throughout the assessment. Stages in completing the evaluability assessment were marked as follows:

— (1/15/80) A briefing on the evaluability assessment goals and process, progress to date, CSP program intent (Task 1 product), and proposed site visits. Review and discussion of products completed to date.

— (4/1/80) A briefing on the actual Community Support Program (Task 2 product), intended to stimulate feedback and reach agreement on program performance indicators.

— (4/28/80) A progress report on Task 3, including discussion of a preliminary list of issues to be considered in assessing the plausibility of CSP objectives and in the development of policy, management, and information options.

— (5/27/80) A report on Tasks 1, 2, and 3, presenting the analysis of findings and preliminary options for changes that would enhance program performance and evaluability. Review and discussion of the options. Report on the addition of two new tasks at the request of CSP management. Extension of the project completion date to June 30, to allow completion of two additional tasks.

Study materials were sent to all policy group members before the briefings. "Prebriefings" were given to CSP program managers before the policy group meetings. Policy group members were briefed and interviewed individually when indicated. Summaries of work group and policy group sessions were distributed to help ensure that members understood feedback received, conclusions reached, decisions made, and planned next steps.

The CSP managers and other policy group members became interested in the evaluability assessment and put evaluability assessment products (for example, the CSP program design model) to use as they were developed. The CSP managers adopted many of the options developed in the evaluability assessment.

## EXAMPLE 3: TENNESSEE'S PRENATAL CARE PROGRAM

This section illustrates the use of evaluability assessment in setting realistic, measurable objectives for a state-level health care program and in identifying priorities for subsequent evaluation work. Here the program was a federally funded demonstration program.

In 1977, in response to high levels of infant morbidity and mortality in Tennessee, the Tennessee Department of Public Health initiated a five-year program, "Toward Improving the Outcome of Pregnancy" (TIOP). The TIOP program was funded through a $400,000 per year grant from the U.S. Department of

Health and Human Services. Funds for expansion of the program came from use of federal formula-grant funds controlled by the Department of Public Health and from a subsequent $300,000 per year federal project grant that allowed expansion of the original three-county TIOP project. Fiscal year 1981 prenatal project expenditures totaled approximately $800,000.

The fiscal year 1981 TIOP program included seven regional projects that provided prenatal care in a total of eighteen counties in Tennessee. Through implementation of model projects in selected "high-risk" areas across the state, TIOP sought to bring together the efforts of state, regional, and local agencies and private providers to develop comprehensive systems for delivery of maternal and infant care. Model projects in local health departments provided community outreach, screening and diagnostic services, treatment, education, and referral and followup of high-risk pregnancies and high-risk infants. In 1982, the Department of Public Health faced the end of the five years of federal funding for TIOP, reductions in other federal funds available to the Department, and likely constraints on the availability of state funding.

The TIOP evaluability assessment, which was initiated and completed in June–July 1981, was the first phase of a thirteen-month evaluation of the TIOP program. The planned TIOP evaluation was to comprise three related efforts: (Part A) evaluation of TIOP in terms of the twelve objectives stated in the original TIOP grant; (Part B) evaluation of the efficiency and effectiveness of TIOP and related prenatal services; (Part C) recommendations on the best follow-through mechanisms once TIOP ended in 1982.

The evaluability assessment was completed by an evaluation team consisting of two staff members from a Department of Public Health contractor (Wholey Associates) and one staff member from the Department's Maternal and Child Health Section. The work of the evaluation team was facilitated by a work group and a policy group established to help guide the evaluation effort. The work group included key central office prenatal program staff and staff from three of the regional TIOP projects; the Policy Group included Maternal and Child Health Section managers, Bureau of Health Services Administration managers, regional office representatives, the Deputy Commissioner of Health, and key budget staff from the Department of Public Health and from the Department of Finance and Administration.[19]

## Documenting the Intended Program

Based on a review of documents, the evaluation team first defined the program envisioned in the twelve objectives stated in the original TIOP grant (see Figure 3-3).

After review of documents describing TIOP and related services and meetings with Department of Public Health personnel, the evaluation team defined the "TIOP and Related Prenatal Care" program as a specific set of resources and activities in the Department of Public Health central office, in the Department's regional health offices, and in nineteen rural county health departments. The team then developed a preliminary program design model. As seen by Department of Public Health policymakers and managers, TIOP and related prenatal care program activities were intended to achieve the objectives presented in Figure 3-4.[20]

Based on feedback from the work group and the policy group, the evaluation team constructed a slightly revised program design model, which guided subsequent evaluation work but was never formally represented to the Department.

After review of Department of Public Health documents, reporting forms, and reports, as well as interaction with central office, regional office, and local health department staff, the evaluation team found that there was broad agreement within the Department on the types of evidence that could be used to assess the performance and results of TIOP and related prenatal care programs. The team identified approximately sixty possible indicators of program performance and results. Quantitative performance indicators were available for most of the events in the Department's prenatal care program design; for example, trimester of pregnancy in which prenatal care was initiated, and infant birthweight. Qualitative performance information could be obtained for other important events; for example, description of interaction with the local medical community. Agreed-on performance indicators were lacking for some of the objectives (for example, provision of prenatal services to "high-risk" patients).

## Documenting Prenatal Care Program Reality

Based on interviews with Department staff, review of many Department of Public Health documents and reports (for example, annual project reports from the regional offices, project budgets

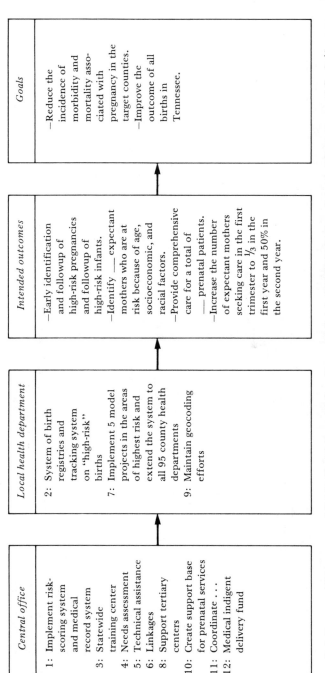

| Central office | Local health department | Intended outcomes | Goals |
|---|---|---|---|
| 1: Implement risk-scoring system and medical record system<br>3: Statewide training center<br>4: Needs assessment<br>5: Technical assistance<br>6: Linkages<br>8: Support tertiary centers<br>10: Create support base for prenatal services<br>11: Coordinate . . . .<br>12: Medical indigent delivery fund | 2: System of birth registries and tracking system on "high-risk" births<br>7: Implement 5 model projects in the areas of highest risk and extend the system to all 95 county health departments<br>9: Maintain geocoding efforts | —Early identification and followup of high-risk pregnancies and followup of high-risk infants.<br>—Identify ___ expectant mothers who are at risk because of age, socioeconomic, and racial factors.<br>—Provide comprehensive care for a total of ___ prenatal patients.<br>—Increase the number of expectant mothers seeking care in the first trimester to $1/3$ in the first year and 50% in the second year. | —Reduce the incidence of morbidity and mortality associated with pregnancy in the target counties.<br>—Improve the outcome of all births in Tennessee. |

**Figure 3–3  Tennessee Department of Public Health Prenatal Care Program:  Original TIOP Objectives, Intended Outcomes, and Goals** (*Source: Joseph S. Wholey and Margaret S. Wholey, Evaluation of TIOP and Related Prenatal Care Programs: Proposed Approach to Parts A, B, and C of the Evaluation* (Arlington, Va.: Wholey Associates, June 1981), p. III–3.)

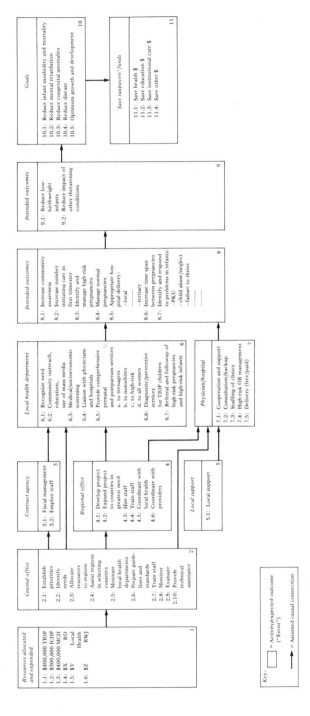

**Figure 3-4   Tennessee Department of Public Health Prenatal Care Program: TIOP, ICHP, and Related Activities** (*Source:* Joseph S. Wholey and Margaret S. Wholey, *Evaluation of TIOP and Related Prenatal Care Programs: Proposed Approach to Parts A, B, and C of the Evaluation* (Arlington, Va.: Wholey Associates, June 1981, pp. III–3a and III–3b).

and expenditure reports, data from the TIOP quarterly reporting system, and annual monitoring reports by central office staff), and a one-day site visit to a prenatal care project, the evaluation team made preliminary assessments of fiscal flows, services being delivered, outcomes of services, and flows of information on the prenatal care program. Analysis of information on the actual program revealed the following:

— The program was providing prenatal care to more than a thousand pregnant women in eighteen rural counties.[21]
— In at least five of these counties, the prenatal care program was serving a significant fraction of all expectant mothers and presumably an even greater fraction of "high-risk" pregnancies.
— Because of restrictions on state funds, replacement of TIOP funds by regional and local funds had not occurred as originally intended. Instead, the regional projects were being supported by federal formula-grant and project-grant funds (much of which would terminate in fiscal year 1982).
— Total public commitments to prenatal care, perinatal care, and related nutrition programs in Tennessee totaled upwards of $20 million per year.
— Most of the intended TIOP services were being provided by central office, regional health offices, contract agencies, local health departments, and private providers. Possible weak spots in the program included the following:

  — Central office and regional offices had had some problems in expanding projects into counties in greatest need (Figure 3-4, Events 2.4 and 4.2).
  — Local health departments appeared to use different definitions of "high-risk" and "need" in determining who would be admitted into the program (Events 6.3, 6.5, and 6.7).
  — Projects had varying success in reaching high-risk women (Event 6.5).
  — Projects appeared to use different criteria in referring high-risk women out of the project for prenatal care by other providers (Events 6.3 and 6.7).
  — Many projects were weak in providing diagnostic and preventive services for TIOP children (Event 6.6).
  — Some projects had had problems in gaining the cooperation and support of physicians and hospitals in certain counties

(Event 7). (In some counties, projects had used additional funds to pay physicians and hospitals part of their normal fees for labor and delivery.)
— Projects were having problems in motivating women to initiate prenatal care in their first trimester of pregnancy (Event 8.2).
— Projects had varying success in identifying and managing high-risk pregnancies (Event 8.3).
— Projects appeared to be generally successful in managing normal pregnancies (Event 8.4).

Based on the information available, none of the objectives appeared to be unrealistic at that point in the evaluation.[22]

## Development of Evaluation Options

Next, the evaluation team developed a set of evaluation options for consideration by the work group and the policy group. Since interviews with Department of Public Health personnel had revealed little demand or anticipated use for additional information on the extent of progress toward the twelve objectives stated in the original TIOP grant, the evaluation team proposed that little evaluation resources be put into Part A of the evaluation. Because interviews with Department of Public Health personnel had revealed a good deal of interest in evaluation of the efficiency and effectiveness of TIOP and because the Department's prenatal care program faced decisions that could have resulted in either reduction or expansion of the program in fiscal year 1982 or 1983, the evaluation team concluded that the Department of Public Health needed six types of evaluation information on the prenatal care program: (1) data on resources expended in TIOP and related programs; (2) data on prenatal and perinatal services delivered; (3) data on service efficiency and productivity; (4) data on outcomes of services (especially on the success of TIOP in stimulating early initiation of prenatal care and in reducing numbers of low-birthweight infants); (5) data on the effectiveness of services in achieving intended outcomes; and (6) data on the cost-effectiveness of prenatal services.

Work group and policy group members were asked to review the proposed list of performance indicators and to indicate their priorities on the specific types of quantitative and qualitative data that were of greatest interest for policy or management use. After the members indicated which types of data were of greatest interest, the evaluation team outlined several sets of comparisons that could be made: (1) TIOP success in meeting statewide standards (for example, moving toward statewide averages); (2) intra-program comparisons among TIOP projects or counties; (3) before and after comparisons and interrupted time series analyses using data on all births in the counties served by TIOP; (4) before and after and interrupted time series comparisons using data on all births in counties served by TIOP and in other counties in the same region not served by TIOP; and (5) before and after and interrupted time series comparisons among TIOP projects offering different services at different costs.

As the evaluation team identified especially effective projects or types of projects, it was proposed that the evaluation team would make site visits to document project resources, services, and service outcomes.[23]

To the extent that time and funds permitted, it was agreed that the evaluation team would examine the existing service delivery system and make recommendations on maintenance and expansion of prenatal services after TIOP funding was to end in fiscal year 1982.

## Decisions on Evaluation Priorities

In early July 1981, the work group and the policy group met (separately) to react to the evaluability assessment. Prebriefings and individual meetings were held with key members of both groups. Work group and policy group reactions to the evaluability assessment resulted in agreement on the following evaluation priorities:

1. *Focus.* The evaluation would focus on the efficiency and effectiveness of TIOP and related prenatal services (Part B of the evaluation). The evaluation would meet Tennessee Department of Public Health needs for the following:

   — data on resources expended in TIOP and related programs
   — data on services delivered
   — data on service efficiency and productivity
   — data on outcomes of services (especially on the success of TIOP in stimulating early initiation of prenatal care and in reducing numbers of low-birthweight infants)

— data on the effectiveness of services in achieving intended outcomes
— data on cost-effectiveness of prenatal services.

2. *Data.* Priority would be given to collection of the following types of data: data on resources expended in TIOP and related programs, numbers of "high-risk" patients (such as teenagers) served, total numbers served, types of services delivered, cost per patient, trimester in which care was initiated, birthweight, qualitative data on identification and management of "high-risk" pregnancies, qualitative data on identification and correction of problems in infants, and qualitative data on projected savings in other programs.

3. *Intended Uses.* The TIOP evaluation was intended to be used in budget decisions for fiscal year 1983, in planning for the prenatal care to be provided in fiscal year 1983 and beyond, in development of formulas for allocation of funds to maintain or expand prenatal services, in reexamination of guidelines and standards for prenatal care, and in regional and local decisions on types of prenatal care to be provided.[24]

These evaluation priorities guided subsequent evaluation work (see Table 3-4).

## Results of the Evaluability Assessment

The evaluability assessment laid the basis for a useful evaluation of Tennessee's prenatal care program. The evaluation team first completed a rapid-feedback evaluation of the Department's prenatal program by November 1981, timed for consideration as part of the preparation of the Governor's proposed fiscal year 1983 budget.[25] The rapid-feedback evaluation pilot-tested specific systems for collecting and analyzing data on the top-priority performance indicators; assessed the performance of TIOP and related prenatal care programs in terms of the agreed-on program performance indicators; suggested that central office and project staff would benefit from ongoing collection, analysis, and use of a small set of indicators of prenatal program accomplishments; and outlined steps to be taken in completing the evaluation.[26]

The rapid-feedback evaluation was used in Tennessee's fiscal

**Table 3–4   TIOP Evaluation Priorities**

| Resources allocated | Services delivered | Short-term outcomes | Longer-term outcomes |
|---|---|---|---|
| 1.1 project $ | 2.1 # admitted | 3.1 trimester care initiated | 4.1 # and % low birthweight (less than 5.5 lbs.) |
| 1.2 $/patient | 2.2 # teenagers admitted | | |
| 1.3 central office guidance, monitoring, and technical assistance | 2.3 # delivered | 3.2 % with appropriate prenatal care | |
| | 2.4 # prenatal clinic visits | | 4.2 % low Apgar score (5-min. less than 8) |
| 1.4 physician/ hospital cooperation and support | 2.5 type prenatal services provided | 3.3 % with late/ no prenatal care | 4.3 perinatal mortality |
| | 2.6 standard used to determine eligibility | 3.4 # delivered with little or no prenatal care (less than 6 visits) | 4.4 infant mortality |
| | 2.7 referrals for high-risk OB management | | 4.5 identification and correction of problems in infants |
| | | 3.5 WIC enrollment | |
| | | 3.6 identification and management of high-risk pregnancies | 4.6 % teenage repeat pregnancies (less than 18 months) |
| | | | 4.7 projected savings in other programs |
| 1.9 resource problems | 2.9 problems with service delivery | 3.9 problems in achieving intended outcomes | 4.9 problems in achieving intended outcomes |

*Source:* Adapted from Joseph S. Wholey and Margaret S. Wholey, *Evaluation of TIOP and Related Prenatal Care Programs: Interim Report* (Arlington, Va.: Wholey Associates, November 1981), p. 5.

year 1983 budget process and in preparation of a Department of Public Health plan for maintenance and expansion of prenatal care throughout Tennessee. Though the budget decisions related primarily to the work of the Governor's Task Force on Mental Retardation Prevention (which had stressed prenatal care), the TIOP evaluation was used in developing formulas for allocating prenatal care funds to regions, in decisions on how prenatal funds would be used, and in developing a plan for managing an expanded prenatal program.

In January 1982, the evaluation team prepared a draft of the management plan later incorporated in the state plan for prenatal services. The proposed management plan included establishment of realistic objectives for improved prenatal care throughout Tennessee; clarification of responsibilities of central office staff, regional health office staff, and local health department staff; specification of information that would be collected to document the extent of prenatal program accomplishments; and suggestions for ways in which program performance information would be used to improve prenatal program performance.[27]

Work group and policy group responses to the rapid-feedback evaluation were used in decisions on the focus of the full-scale evaluation and in decisions on the assistance to be provided by the evaluation team in planning for an expanded prenatal program: work on the management plan for an expanded and improved prenatal program; work on simpler, more timely systems for regional and county reporting on health department services and on outcomes of pregnancy; work on a simpler, more timely system for central office summary and feedback of comparative data to regions and to county health departments; and exploration of possibilities for gaining additional Medicaid and WIC nutrition program resources for prenatal patients.[28]

## ISSUES, PROBLEMS, AND SOLUTIONS: LESSONS LEARNED ON EVALUABILITY ASSESSMENT

As this and the next chapter suggest, the products of evaluability assessment are valued by government managers at many levels. In the remainder of this chapter we examine issues and problems that arise in doing evaluability assessments, and outline solutions based on past experience with evaluability assessment.[29]

## Gaining and Holding the Cooperation and Support of Managers

Evaluators typically take a long time to do their work, while the time scales of their intended audiences tend to be highly compressed. Moreover, it takes time to gain managers' confidence and to produce program change. Evaluators need mechanisms that will convince managers that it is worth their while to become and stay engaged in the evaluation process.

Getting off to a good start can be a problem. At a minimum, evaluators should begin an evaluability assessment by clarifying the types of products and results expected from the assessment.

By quickly providing objective, credible information relevant to problems that managers face, the evaluability assessment process tends to overcome managers' skepticism. As the Civil Service Reform and Community Support Program examples show, the stages in an evaluability assessment facilitate the briefings and discussions needed to keep evaluators' work relevant to management needs. Each such briefing can be used to present a preliminary evaluability assessment product (for example, the program design model, findings from site visits, or options for program change) and to elicit the management feedback needed to reach agreement on a revised product or to identify a need for collection of additional data. These meetings allow the evaluator to determine which managers want and need information, allowing the evaluator to test the market for subsequent evaluation work by presenting relevant information based on very small samples of data on program performance.

## Clarifying Program Intent

Program design models can be developed at varying levels of detail. These models help to develop a common understanding between managers and evaluators on intended program activities, intended outcomes, and assumed causal linkages: a prerequisite for evaluation work that is likely to be useful to management. The program design models display, in shorthand form, all the relevant evaluations that could be conducted, since they display the key events that could be monitored and the assumed causal linkages that could be tested in evaluations of the program. (The program design models are likely to evolve during an evaluability assessment, as the evaluator learns more about management's expectations for the program and as management makes decisions that may alter the intended program design.)

The question here is one of the appropriate level of detail in the program design model. More detailed program design models, like Figures 3-1 and 3-4, are useful in ensuring that the evaluator has a clear understanding of the program and that both evaluators and managers have a common understanding of the way in which the program is intended to achieve its results. These models are best communicated in papers that managers and staff can study before meeting with the evaluator.

For briefings and discussions with higher management and policy levels, less detailed program design models may be more appropriate (see, for example, Figure 2-5). Simpler program design models allow the evaluator to focus briefings and discussions on key issues. They also facilitate clear distinctions between those program objectives for which management will take responsibility and those for which they will not.

## Documenting the Actual Program

The second phase of the evaluability assessment is carried out to document (a slice of) program reality. In some evaluability assessments, however, efforts to document the actual program have resulted only in additional, more detailed models of intended program activities and outcomes. In many other cases, site visit reports have taken a long time to prepare but have yielded little useful information.

The evaluators' reviews of actual flows of resources (staff time and money), grant applications, project reports, monitoring reports, and the like, as well as the evaluators' site visits, are intended to provide the bases for development of valid measures of program performance, evidence as to the likelihood that program objectives will be achieved, and bases for development of program change options. The evaluators' activities in this phase should therefore focus on descriptions of project activities actually occurring and project outcomes actually being achieved; reviews of all program and project measurement systems currently in use; descriptions of especially strong project performance and of problems inhibiting strong project performance; and collection of project estimates of likely accomplishments over the next few years.[30]

## Assessing the Likelihood of Effective Program Performance

In evaluability assessment, a key step is the evaluator's assessment of the likelihood that program objectives will be achieved. Successful completion of this step requires a modest amount of contact with program reality: firsthand contact, through relatively small numbers of site visits and interviews; and secondhand contact, through analyses of grant applications, program expenditures, project reports, monitoring reports, audits, past research and evaluation studies, information from knowledgeable observers of the program, and so on.

Reviews of successful and unsuccessful evaluability assessments strongly suggest that a small number of site visits are needed early in the assessment. Guided by a preliminary version of the program design model, the evaluators can gather needed information about actual levels of resources, program activities actually under way, program outcomes actually occurring, and trouble spots that seem to be emerging. The evaluators can then make judgments as to the likelihood that program objectives will be achieved.

New information from the field gives the evaluability assessment credibility. The "early warning" nature of the plausibility analysis allows the evaluators to raise problems in the program design while there is still time for management to act. And information from the site visits strongly influences the development of options for program change.

## Identifying Options for Changes in Program Resources, Activities, or Objectives

Reviews of successful and unsuccessful evaluability assessments suggest the need to develop program change options more than once: initially, to get preliminary management reactions as to which options are worth pursuing; and subsequently, to spell out options in sufficient detail to allow informed management commitments and effective implementation of the options selected. An important part of the job of spelling out program change options, therefore, is that of clarifying the costs of the program change options in terms of dollars, staff time, management time, and other resources.[31]

In a number of the more successful evaluability assessment efforts, continual interaction between evaluators and managers has led to agreement on implementation work needed to make one or more of the options effective. These implementation activities were either incorporated as additional tasks in the evaluability assessment (as in the Community Support Program example) or commissioned as specific follow-on activities by the evaluation team (as in the Civil Service Reform and the Prenatal Care Program examples).

## Developing Information Options

As we will suggest in Chapter 5, a good deal of contact with program reality is required for development of valid measures of program performance. Reviews of program monitoring reports, reviews of project reports, and site visits allow the evaluator to construct typologies of program activities and outcomes that can serve as bases for development of valid program performance measures.

As in the policy and management options, the information options should include estimates of the costs of the options. For information options, the relevant costs will be the costs of collecting, analyzing, and using specific types of program performance data.[32] In addition, information options should include hypothetical or real examples of the data that would be made available and specific indications of how that information would be used.

## Getting Policy and Management Decisions

The most important step in evaluability assessment is getting management decisions on the set of program objectives and performance indicators in terms of which they will assess and manage the program.[33] Some evaluability assessments have failed, however, to get management decisions on program objectives, program activities, or the collection and use of information.

The keys to getting the necessary policy and management decisions appear to be (1) holding the interest of management through provision of early evaluability assessment products; (2) continuing interaction with management at frequent intervals; (3) briefing key individuals on evaluability assessment findings and options to clarify the findings and options and to get their positions on the options; and (4) providing the additional information needed to clarify the options and prepare for implementation of the highest-priority options.

The Civil Service Reform and Community Support Program assessments resulted in management actions designed to improve program performance; the Civil Service Reform, Community Support Program and Prenatal Care Program assessments all resulted in management decisions on program objectives and information priorities. As in these examples, when the evaluability assessment is the initial phase of a larger evaluation effort or a mechanism is available for speedy initiation of follow-on work, implementation of management decisions is more likely.

## Documenting Policy and Management Decisions

Some evaluability assessments have failed to document policy and management decisions on the objectives and performance indicators in terms of which the program is to be assessed and managed.[34] In each of the evaluability assessment examples discussed in this chapter, the evaluators found it helpful to conclude each phase of the assessment with a brief memo indicating significant policy and management decisions reached in group or individual meetings.

## Proceeding by Successive Iterations

All too often, evaluators exhaust the resources available for evaluability assessments without achieving management decisions on the objectives on which the program is to be held accountable, the types of information to be used to assess progress toward those objectives, or intended uses of program performance information.

The evaluability assessment can often be brought to a more timely, more successful conclusion by accomplishing the assessment by successive iterations. When using this strategy, the evaluators first do the entire evaluability assessment (all the steps) once in the initial weeks of the assessment; obtain tentative management decisions on program objectives, program activities, and collection and use of information; and then redo some or all of the evaluability assessment as often as necessary to achieve informed management decisions and a better-designed program. Each iteration of the evaluability assessment allows the evaluator both to provide new information to management and to better sense management's positions as to which options appear most feasible and useful.[35]

## Reducing Evaluability Assessment Costs

Schmidt, Beyna, and Haar have estimated that contracted evaluability assessments of Department of Health and Human Services programs have cost between $50,000 and $120,000, plus additional effort by in-house work groups and project officers, and have taken between three and ten calendar months. They estimate that in-house HHS evaluability assessments have required six to eighteen staff-months of effort and three to ten calendar months.[36] In the Tennessee Department of Public Health, evaluability assessment of a fairly simple, fairly well-documented program cost $11,000 plus several staff-days of effort by in-house work group members and the project officer; it required only seven calendar weeks to complete. Schmidt, Beyna, and Haar note that more complex programs generally require more effort, and that more effort will be required when less information is available on past program performance. They also suggest that fewer people working full time are more efficient than more people working part time.

Earlier writings on evaluability assessment have been heavily procedural, requiring the evaluator to produce many intermediate written products. In addition to consuming time that could better be used in briefings and discussions with program managers and their staffs, the intermediate written products have sometimes gotten in the way of good communication among evaluators, managers, and staff. In this book and other recent writings on evaluability assessment, evaluators are emphasizing the spirit of the evaluability assessment approach, concentrating on those products actually required for management decisions. Focusing on essentials makes the evaluability assessment process more efficient and thus reduces its costs.

## CONCLUSION

In this and the preceding chapter we have explored an approach through which evaluators can help managers and policymakers to come to agreement on sets of realistic, measurable objectives in terms of which programs will be assessed and managed. Before examining some relatively inexpensive methods for assessing program performance (Chapters 5-7), in Chapter 4 we will review evidence on managers' reactions to the evaluability assessment process and products.

## NOTES TO CHAPTER 3

1. Richard Schmidt provided helpful comments on an earlier draft of this chapter.

2. Leonard Rutman has been responsible for much of the progress in evaluability assessment in Canada; the U.S. Department of Education has made extensive use of evaluability assessment even in an uncertain policy environment. See Leonard Rutman, *Planning Useful Evaluations: Evaluability Assessment* (Beverly Hills, Calif.: Sage Publications, 1980); Treasury Board of Canada, Comptroller General, *Guide on the Program Evaluation Function* (Ottawa: Minister of Supply and Services Canada, 1981); and the series of papers presented by Steven M. Jung and his American Institutes of Research colleagues at the March 1982 American Educational Research Association symposium on Department of Education evaluability assessments.

3. The account in this section is based on the following: Mark A. Abramson, "Summary Report: Evaluability Assessment of the Senior Executive Service in the Department of Health and Human Services," U.S. Department of Health and Human Services working paper, January 1981 (draft); Mark A. Abramson and Sandra Baxter, "The Senior Executive Service: A Preliminary Assessment from One Department" (Paper presented at the Symposium on

Changing Public Bureaucracy: Civil Service Reform Three Years Later, State University of New York at Binghamton, October 28-29, 1981); Mark A. Abramson and others, "Evaluating a Personnel System: The Civil Service Reform Act of 1978, A Case Study," *Review of Public Personnel Administration*, Spring 1982; Bruce Buchanan, "The Senior Executive Service: How We Can Tell If It Works," *Public Administration Review*, vol. 41, no. 3 (May/June 1981), pp. 349-358; Richard E. Schmidt, "Evaluability Assessment and Cost Analysis," in Marvin Alkin, ed., *Costs of Evaluation* (Beverly Hills, Calif.: Sage Publications, in press); and working papers prepared as part of the Senior Executive Service evaluability assessment.

4. *The Civil Service Reform Act of 1978*, P.L. 95-454 (October 13, 1978).

5. Abramson, "Summary Report."

6. Ibid.

7. Ibid.

8. Abramson and others, "Evaluating a Personnel System."

9. Memorandum from Joe Wholey, Deputy Assistant Secretary for Evaluation, U.S. Department of Health, Education, and Welfare, "Management Options for the HEW SES Program," May 2, 1980.

10. A good discussion of the process that produced the agreed-on evaluation design appears in Schmidt, "Evaluability Assessment and Cost Analysis."

11. Abramson and Baxter, "The Senior Executive Service," Appendix.

12. Abramson, "Summary Report." Also see Abramson and others, "Evaluating a Personnel System."

13. The account in this section is based on the following: Beth Stroul and others, *Final Report of the Exploratory Evaluation of the National Institute of Mental Health Community Support Program* (Silver Spring, Md.: Macro Systems, 1980); Office of the Assistant Secretary for Planning and Evaluation, U.S. Department of Health and Human Services, *Report on Evaluation Utilization in the Department of Health and Human Services* (Washington, D.C.: 1981), pp. 32-33; and J. Richard Woy, National Institute of Mental Health, "Evaluability Assessment: Method of the Moment," August 1981 (draft).

14. Stroul and others, *Final Report*.

15. Ibid.

16. *Report on Evaluation Utilization*, pp. 32-33.

17. Ibid.

18. Woy, "Evaluability Assessment."

19. "TIOP Evaluation Work Group . . .; TIOP Evaluation Policy Group," Tennessee Department of Public Health working paper, n.d. (1981).

20. Joseph S. Wholey and Margaret S. Wholey, *Evaluation of TIOP and Related Prenatal Care Programs: Proposed Approach to Parts A, B, and C of the Evaluation*, Report prepared for the Tennessee Department of Public Health (Arlington, Va.: Wholey Associates, June 1981), p. III-2.

21. Subsequent evaluation work showed that the program was serving approximately 1,670 patients per year.

22. Wholey and Wholey, *Proposed Approach*, p. V-4.

23. Ibid., p. VI–4.

24. Memorandum from Joe and Midge Wholey, Wholey Associates, "Design for Evaluation of TIOP and Related Prenatal Care Programs," July 27, 1981.

25. Rapid-feedback evaluation is discussed in Chapter 5.

26. Joseph S. Wholey and Margaret S. Wholey, *Evaluation of TIOP and Related Prenatal Care Programs: Interim Report*, Report prepared for the Tennessee Department of Public Health (Arlington, Va.: Wholey Associates, November 1981).

27. Memorandum from Joe and Midge Wholey, Wholey Associates, "Prenatal Plan," January 16, 1982.

28. Memorandum from Joe and Midge Wholey, Wholey Associates, "Next Steps in the TIOP Evaluation," January 19, 1982.

29. This section is based on two Department of Health and Human Services (HHS) workshops on evaluability assessment (December 1979 and July 1980); a summary of responses from HHS evaluability assessment contractors by Richard E. Schmidt, U.S. Department of Health and Human Services, May 14, 1981; John W. Scanlon and James Bell, *Short Term Study of Evaluability Assessment Activity in the Public Health Service*, Report prepared for the Office of the Assistant Secretary for Health, U.S. Department of Health and Human Services, 1981; and the author's experience with evaluability assessment over the past several years.

30. See John W. Scanlon and James Bell, "Participant's Notebook : E&TA Workshop on Evaluability Assessment," Paper prepared for the Office of the Assistant Secretary for Planning and Evaluation, U.S. Department of Health and Human Services (Washington, D.C.: Performance Development Institute, 1980), Figure 2.

31. See Richard Schmidt, Larry Beyna, and Jerry Haar, "Evaluability Assessment: Principles and Practice," in Gerald J. Stahler and William R. Tash, eds., *Innovative Approaches to Mental Health Evaluation* (New York: Academic Press, 1982), pp. 195–219.

32. A good discussion of the development of information options appears in Schmidt, "Evaluability Assessment and Cost Analysis."

33. See Scanlon and Bell, "Participant's Notebook."

34. Scanlon and Bell, *Short Term Study*, pp. 8-9.

35. John W. Scanlon and James Bell, HHS Workshop on Evaluability Assessment, U.S. Department of Health and Human Services, Washington, D.C., July 25, 1980.

36. Schmidt, Beyna, and Haar, "Evaluability Assessment," p. 217.

# 4

# Management Uses
# of Evaluability
# Assessment

## INTRODUCTION

Since its early stages of development in 1973, evaluability assessment has been used in countless settings at federal, state, and local levels in this country and in Canada. In Canada, for example, Leonard Rutman has helped the Office of the Auditor General to implement evaluability assessment in many agencies.[1] Sharon Studer has noted the usefulness of an early version of evaluability assessment as it was applied by an evaluation unit attached to the Minnesota state legislature.[2]

In this chapter we will be particularly interested in examining evidence on the usefulness of evaluability assessment as a management tool. Its biggest test has been in the U.S. Department of Health, Education, and Welfare (HEW), which is now the Department of Health and Human Services (HHS). Between 1978 and 1980 the Department conducted a demonstration effort to encourage the use of evaluability assessment as an initial step in improving the usefulness of evaluation to managers throughout the Department. Using in-house staff and six contractors, the Office of the Assistant Secretary for Planning and Evaluation (ASPE) conducted approximately twenty-five evaluability assessments over the two-year period, most of them in the Public Health Service and the U.S. Office of Education (now the Department of Education). By the end of the demonstration period, the Public Health Service and the Department of Education decided to initiate their

own evaluability assessments to help program managers and policymakers to clarify program objectives and agree on appropriate
program performance indicators.

In this chapter we review intended uses of evaluability assessment, problems in getting evaluability assessment results used, and
steps toward solution of those problems. We then present the findings of follow-up studies in the U.S. Department of Health and
Human Services. The chapter includes feedback from Public
Health Service managers and executives who were directly involved in evaluability assessments.

## INTENDED USES OF EVALUABILITY ASSESSMENT

Evaluability assessments provide three types of information: (1)
information on the extent of agreement on program objectives,
priorities, and types of evidence that would indicate success; (2)
information on deficiencies in program performance and opportunities to improve program performance; and (3) information on
deficiencies in collection and use of program performance data
and opportunities for change.

Evaluability assessment can help managers and policymakers
by promoting greater understanding of differences in program
intent, of differences between program intent and program reality,
and of differences between program reality and the types of information available on program performance.

At a minimum, evaluability assessment hopes to promote informed policy and management decisions on the collection and
use of program performance data. The evaluability assessment will
have studied existing program monitoring, reporting, and evaluation systems, and will have collected qualitative and quantitative
data from at least a few local projects. With this information and
information on policymakers' and managers' information needs,
those conducting the evaluability assessment should be in position
to outline cost-feasible systems for assessing program performance
and to determine ways in which performance monitoring and
other types of evaluation could inform policy decisions and contribute to improved program performance.

Further, evaluability assessment hopes to stimulate changes in program activities that will contribute to improved program performance.

## PROBLEMS IN GETTING EVALUABILITY ASSESSMENT RESULTS USED; STEPS TOWARD SOLUTIONS

All those who conduct evaluability assessments face four potential problems: (1) the evaluators may fail to get the attention of managers and policymakers; (2) the evaluators may fail to produce information that is sufficiently relevant and conclusive to be useful; (3) the evaluators may fail to identify policy, management, or information options that are feasible; and (4) as a result of other pressures and concerns, managers and policymakers may simply fail to act.

As we saw in Chapters 2 and 3, evaluability assessment is designed to overcome these problems by involving policymakers, managers, and program staff; by producing credible new information; and by identifying problems and solutions of interest to policymakers, managers, and program staff. Still, implementation failures may occur.

Over the last three years, evaluators in the Department of Health and Human Services and in the Department of Education have modified the evaluability assessment process to facilitate the conduct and use of evaluability assessment. Both departments have used policy groups and work groups to facilitate policy-level, management, and staff involvement, decision making, and implementation of needed changes:

— For a specific evaluability assessment, the *work group* consists of program and policy staff knowledgeable about the program and able to contribute information that will focus the evaluability assessment efforts and keep them relevant. The work work group stays involved throughout the evaluability assessment.
— The *policy group* for an evaluability assessment consists of higher-level managers and policymakers who individually and collectively influence the program. The policy group is briefed periodically on evaluability assessment findings and options.

Although both groups slow the evaluability assessment process somewhat, they provide ongoing information and involvement that help make the evaluability assessment successful. Of the two, the work groups are usually more helpful. In some cases, the policy groups are less helpful because of the fragmented nature of policy-level authority and because policy-level people are not accustomed to making decisions designed to improve program performance.

Whether work groups, policy groups, or meetings with individuals are used, some method of ensuring policymaker and management involvement is necessary to the success of the evaluability assessment's consensus-building effort. Presentations of evaluability-assessment findings, for example, include steps designed to overcome the problem listed above:

— The content of evaluability assessment presentations includes information clarifying problems, possible policy and management solutions, and ways in which program performance information could be used.
— The evaluability assessment process includes individual briefings to key managers and policymakers to clarify findings, to supply more information when necessary, and to ascertain the priorities of individual decision makers prior to group decision sessions. The process also includes meetings with relevant decision makers as a group in order to build consensus and to reach decisions on the priority objectives on which the program will be held accountable, on important side effects that will also be monitored, on the performance indicators that will be used, and on the changes in program activities that will be made to improve program performance.

## POLICY AND MANAGEMENT USES OF EVALUABILITY ASSESSMENT

Department of Health and Human Services (HHS) staff have documented policy and management uses of several of the evaluability assessments completed by in-house staff and contractors in 1979 and 1980. The uses identified include the following: setting more realistic program objectives, policy and management changes to correct problems and deficiencies, and establishing frameworks for evaluation and analysis. The following examples were among the specific uses documented:

1. The Federal Council on the Aging used an evaluability assessment of Administration on Aging (AoA) programs to choose a policy focus for a congressionally-mandated study of the Older Americans Act programs.[3]
2. The Senior Executive Service (SES) evaluability assessment resulted in agreement on a set of objectives and performance indicators for the HHS SES Program and the design of a full-scale evaluation of the program. In addition, on the basis of periodic briefings throughout the evaluability assessment, several substantive actions were taken, including the following:

   — To fill a gap between departmental objectives and individual performance plans, the Secretary issued a directive mandating linkage between objectives in the Department's Operational Management System and the Department's performance appraisal system.
   — To make the SES system more equitable, the Assistant Secretary for Personnel Administration developed a system that would take degree of job difficulty into account in determining the size of SES bonuses.
   — To increase support within the SES, the Assistant Secretary for Personnel Administration initiated SES information exchange conferences and an SES newsletter.
   — To make the Department's personnel system more equitable, a bonus award system was proposed for noncareer SES members, who are not eligible for SES bonuses per se.[4]

3. Evaluability assessment of the Rehabilitation Services Administration (RSA) program resulted in management actions to improve Rehabilitation Services Administration effectiveness in ensuring uniform compliance with the Vocational Rehabilitation (VR) legislation; to improve RSA effectiveness in stimulating state VR agency efforts to improve the VR program according to nationally defined priorities; and to improve the RSA policy development and dissemination role.[5]

## MANAGEMENT USES OF EVALUABILITY ASSESSMENT IN THE PUBLIC HEALTH SERVICE (PHS)

In a study for the Office of the Assistant Secretary for Health (OASH) and the Office of the Assistant Secretary for Planning and Evaluation (ASPE) in the U.S. Department of Health and Human Services, John Scanlon and James Bell examined evaluability assessments of ten Public Health Service Programs. These evaluability assessments (EAs) constituted a purposefully selected sample of the forty Public Health Service evaluability assessments completed or ongoing as of July 1980. The sample included at least one evaluability assessment from each of the five Public Health Service agencies involved in evaluability assessment; it contained both evaluability assessments believed to have achieved high utilization and evaluability assessments for which utilization was believed less likely.[6] This study provides extensive documentation of managers' views on evaluability assessment.

In this study Scanlon and Bell discussed the evaluability assessments (EAs) with the relevant program managers, with planning and evaluation office managers, and (where possible) with executives who had line authority over the programs. The Scanlon-Bell study was intended to assess whether the evaluability assessment products had met expectations and whether the evaluability assessment process was likely to continue in the Public Health Service. As a result of their study, Scanlon and Bell arrived at the following conclusions:

— The EAs reviewed did produce information and results, but not all the products called for in the ASPE manual.[7]
— Program managers and executives involved in the EAs were satisfied and indicated their willingness to recommend EA and participate in future EAs (12 of 12 in the sample).
— Program managers involved in EA acknowledged using the EA products and could describe those uses (7 out of 9).
— Continuation of EAs by the five agencies in the study is likely. . . .[8]

Based on review of five of the evaluability assessments and interviews on all ten, Scanlon and Bell concluded that PHS evaluability assessments tended to produce information documenting the intended program, documenting the actual program, and assessing the evaluability of the program; however, they tended not to document the program managers' decisions on performance measures and program design.[9]

Scanlon and Bell noted that all the program managers and executives involved in evaluability assessments were positive about evaluability assessment. Among the comments of the executives were the following:

— "I would recommend EA in certain situations. Properly done, in the right situation it is valuable. . . . I'm not sure everything would lend itself to EA. For new programs it makes sense."[10]

— "I'd recommend EA, especially for a new program. . . . It is worthwhile in the following way—it enables program people, over time, to sharpen objectives and change them. . . . Now I expect [from EA] a very clear set of objectives that are meaningful, realistic, quantitative, and described over time."[11]

— "Besides helping the program managers, some of the EAs helped me to make important judgments about program performance. In turn, the EAs helped in my dialogues with the Secretary about the programs. I recommend EA as one of a small number of techniques that really helped us get a better handle on program performance. . . . SDAs [service delivery assessments] and our inhouse program reviews are other techniques that proved helpful."[12]

The program managers had comments like these:

— "I am satisfied with it and used it. Yes, I would recommend it. . . . EA is good for any managed activity. . . . EA is not a traditional evaluation tool. EA develops information where I [can] act. . . . I expect an EA to gather information from all sources objectively and to do a critical analysis of perceptions and relationships in order to determine whether and if they are congruent with goals."[13]

— "This project [EA] is enormously useful. It is the first time that the scientific community, program staff and planners have worked together to develop proposals for change and improvement. . . . It's the first time in my eight years here that we have been able to look five years down the road. We have been able to analyze our fiscal situation — given the constraints on budget, which options are most feasible. . . . It is very helpful to my staff and me to see what we are all about."[14]

— "Relative to the muscle put into it, I was satisfied with the EA. It seems like a good deal in comparison to other purchases. . . . If I were put in charge of a new program with a well accepted goal, I'd use EA to design the program's service delivery mechanism. I wouldn't use EA if I knew the program was troubled by longstanding, difficult policy questions."[15]

Scanlon and Bell discovered that the executives and managers were far more positive about evaluability assessment than about evaluation in general, which the executives and managers viewed as not being either timely or relevant to their concerns. They identified three characteristics of evaluability assessment that seemed to attract managers: (1) quality information that is produced quickly; (2) useable products; (3) the fact that the process creates a forum for discussion.[16]

In open-ended interviews, seven of the nine program managers and three of the three executives involved in evaluability assessments stated that they found evaluability assessment useful. These managers and executives described six types of uses they made of evaluability products:

— Identified the need to change authorizing legislation and helped justify proposed amendments (one program manager).
— Set more realistic objectives, developed priorities (two program managers, two executives).
— Directed staff to correct problems and deficiencies (four program managers, two executives).
— Led policy levels to understand the program and set more realistic policies and budgets (two program managers).
— Informed people up and down the line on program objectives and design, in order to get shared understanding and consensus (four program managers).
— Established a design/framework for evaluation and analysis (three program managers).

Scanlon and Bell noted that, since the managers and executives were not systematically taken through a checklist of these uses, these responses represent minimum levels of each type of use.[17]

Reactions from the executives were along the following lines:

— "The EA was indeed useful. It pointed out that we were too optimistic. The problem and the program are not as simple as we thought. There are no State data bases and systems out there as in our other programs. . . . Things are happening as a result. We have concluded that we need more effort on the data systems . . . we can't go far with a demonstration without dealing with that."[18]
— "EA is useful with a State-Federal model. States want assistance. They are so anxious to get it, they don't pay much attention to examination of objectives that the Federal people are selling. This process brings

federal and State people closer together in the real world. That is unusual. I've seen many State-Federal programs that generally do not have realistic expectations. EA helps make them realistic."[19]

— "The findings from the EA confirmed our fears that the program was not going to live up to Congressional expectations. It helped to set in motion some of the remedial actions we took."[20]

## The program managers had the following kinds of reactions:

— "EA made the policy group come to terms with the logic. They agreed to the steps required to have impact. Now I can point out where I have a lack of resources to carry out logic. If they say no resources then there will be no impact. I couldn't have these discussions without the logic model. For three years I have been frustrated in these discussions because different policy people will only deal with their part and ignore all other parts. . . . I am using the EA to prepare [an] option paper for policy discussions about planned cuts in the program. . . . I made the EA required reading for everyone in the program. I am printing 100 copies for dissemination to States, Regional Offices and headquarters."[21]

— "I never received useful information. . . . We desperately needed what they said they were going to do. We had to respond to OMS [the Secretary's management-by-objectives system]. In truth, we set up our own [study]. We are tracking the program on the OMS measures. May not be related to what should be, but in a crises [sic] we had to do something. . . . I haven't the foggiest idea where it is now."[22]

— "As I got information I would act to change things. I was getting a short term evaluation of the functioning of the program. . . . I used the feedback process most. It enabled us to get a collective understanding of a same direction; to get a reasonable degree of consensus on direction in my office and in the regions."[23]

— "We realized through EA that our goals were too broad so we revised planning guidance to the field agencies to focus on four core areas. . . . We needed to get better coordination among central office managers and the EA process brought them together over issues related to the long term performance of the program. . . . We wanted to amend the act after the EA helped show a preoccupation with planning in the field. Results from the EA helped us to get the amendment."[24]

— "The findings were new to me, but they allowed me to dialogue about the findings with superiors in a non-crisis atmosphere. The findings helped me deflect [our director's] penchant to add commitments to states on our already overloaded program. We did revise our grant announcement to give grantees more latitude and used EA products in the process."[25]

— "EA [led] to important shifts in our program. I think it helped to refine the program design. We changed content of grant announcement, established a framework for future evaluation and analysis."[26]

## CONCLUSION

Evaluability assessment is one way to get policy and management agreement on a set of objectives and performance indicators in terms of which a program is to be assessed and managed. In some cases, evaluability assessments produce sufficient information to stimulate policy and management decisions designed to improve program performance.

In the next three chapters we will examine three other relatively inexpensive methods for evaluating program performance: rapid-feedback evaluation, service delivery assessment, and outcome monitoring. Each of these approaches can provide relevant, useful, preliminary evaluations at relatively low cost; each can lay the basis for more conclusive full-scale evaluations.

## NOTES TO CHAPTER 4

1. See Leonard Rutman, *Planning Useful Evaluations: Evaluability Assessment* (Beverly Hills, Calif.: Sage Publications, 1980). Also see Treasury Board of Canada, Comptroller General, *Guide to the Program Evaluation Function* (Ottawa: Minister of Supply and Services Canada, 1981).

2. Sharon Studer, "Evaluation Needs Assessments: Can They Make Evaluation Work?" *The Bureaucrat*, vol. 9, no. 4 (Winter 1980–81), pp. 14–21. Studer's paper suggested the need to give greater emphasis to the spirit of the evaluability assessment approach, as opposed to earlier expositions of evaluability assessment as an "eight-step process." I have responded to this suggestion in Chapters 2 and 3.

3. Office of the Assistant Secretary for Planning and Evaluation, U.S. Department of Health and Human Services, *Summaries of Completed Evaluation Studies* (n.d.).

4. Ibid. The Senior Executive Service evaluability assessment was presented in Chapter 3.

5. Ibid.

6. John W. Scanlon and James Bell, *Short Term Study of Evaluability Assessment Activity in the Public Health Service*, Report prepared for the Office of the Assistant Secretary for Health, U.S. Department of Health and Human Services, Washington, D.C., May 1981, p. 5.

7. The ASPE Manual referred to is Richard E. Schmidt, John W. Scanlon, and James B. Bell, *Evaluability Assessment: Making Public Programs Work Better* (Rockville, Md.: U.S. Department of Health, Education, and Welfare, Project Share, Human Services Monograph No. 14, 1979).

8. Scanlon and Bell, *Short Term Study*, p. 4.

9. Ibid., pp. 8–12.
10. Ibid., p. B–2.
11. Ibid.
12. Ibid. (Service delivery assessment will be examined in Chapter 6.)
13. Ibid.
14. Ibid., p. B–3.
15. Ibid.
16. Ibid., pp. 14–15.
17. Ibid., p. 17.
18. Ibid., p. D–2.
19. Ibid.
20. Ibid.
21. Ibid.
22. Ibid., p. D–3.
23. Ibid.
24. Ibid.
25. Ibid., p. D–4.
26. Ibid.

PART

Assessing
Program
Performance
and Results

# 5

## Developing Performance Measures and Evaluation Designs

## INTRODUCTION

Chapters 2-4 showed the importance of obtaining policy and management agreement on the objectives and performance indicators in terms of which a program is to be assessed and managed. They suggested a process, evaluability assessment, through which evaluators and other analysts can help create the necessary agreement; and they examined the usefulness of that process to government managers. Assuming policy and management agreement on a set of program objectives and program performance indicators, this chapter suggests how to develop a system for assessing program performance in terms of those objectives and performance indicators. In particular, the chapter describes an evaluation method, *rapid-feedback evaluation,* that provides a quick preliminary assessment of program performance as part of the process of developing program performance measures and designing a full-scale evaluation.[1]

Given a framework of agreed-on, outcome-oriented program objectives, design of a system for assessing program performance requires specification of several elements:

1. The program performance measures to be used: agreed-on program performance indicators, data sources, data collection methods, data collection instruments or questionnaires, sampling design, and sample size.

2. The comparisons to be made: nonexperimental designs, quasi-experimental designs, or experimental designs.
3. The intended uses of program performance information.
4. The resources to be committed to data collection, data analysis, and information dissemination and utilization.
5. Work plans and schedules for data collection, data analysis, and information dissemination and utilization.

In this chapter we explore the first two elements: measurements and comparisons. Two examples of rapid-feedback evaluation are presented to demonstrate the usefulness of preliminary evaluations based on small samples and to suggest measurement schemes that will be useful in evaluation of many public programs.


## DEVELOPING PERFORMANCE MEASURES

Specification of program performance measures requires specification of (1) the performance indicators (types of evidence) to be used to assess program performance; (2) specification of data sources, data collection methods, and data collection instruments or questionnaires; and (3) specification of sampling design and sample size. The goal is production of program performance data that are relevant, valid, reliable, and not too costly.


### Program Performance Indicators

This chapter assumes that, through evaluability assessment or other means, policy and management agreement has been reached on the performance indicators (types of evidence) to be used to assess program performance.

John Scanlon has noted that appropriate program performance indicators can often be developed from existing informal systems for assessing program performance: If a program has a site-visit monitoring system, for example, the evaluator might develop program performance indicators by making more explicit the standards used by individual monitors and getting management reactions as to whether any differences in standards constitute a problem. Scanlon has also suggested that evaluators can develop local operations, getting management reactions as to which of the local activities and results are good or bad, and creating typologies that will allow efficient communication of program performance and results.[2]

## Data Sources, Data Collection Methods, and
## Data Collection Instruments

The most important sources of program performance data are agency and program records, existing data systems, direct observations, and special surveys.

To support results-oriented management, it will usually be necessary to collect program outcome data that go beyond the input and process data typically found in program records and administrative monitoring systems but are closer to program activities than the social indicators (mortality rates, unemployment rates, and crime rates, for example) reported in standard statistical series. Collection of program outcome data will often require special surveys or site visits. (A side benefit of site visits and surveys is that they put less burden on subordinate units than do typical program reporting systems.)

### Telephone Surveys

Given agreement on the types of evidence to be used to assess program performance and results, telephone surveys can quickly provide relevant data on attitudes, opinions, and experiences of those involved in the program. The speed with which telephone surveys can be completed should recommend the technique to those attempting to meet the accelerated time schedules of managers and policymakers.

Telephone surveys typically provide data at approximately one-third the cost of personal interviews.[3] The feasibility of repeated call-backs makes it possible to achieve the high response rates (at least 80 percent) required to ensure valid estimates of program performance. Use of centralized telephone banks makes it fairly easy for survey supervisors to ensure data quality by closely monitoring those collecting the data. Spiraling costs have put limits on the amount of personal interviewing that is practical. A good deal of research has shown that a changeover to telephone surveys can reduce survey costs without reducing the validity of survey data.[4]

Though telephone surveys are widely used in market research, political polling, and production of social indicators like the unemployment rate, telephone surveys are still underutilized in program monitoring and evaluation. At the Urban Institute, on the contrary, staff members often use telephone surveys; for example, in assessing the performance and results of housing, education, technical assistance, police paraprofessional, team policing, and mental health programs.[5] Later in this chapter we describe the use of telephone surveys in collecting data on the performance of a large planning and regulatory program.

*Site Visits*

Site visiting is a traditional administrative monitoring technique. Site-visit reports can convey the reality of program operations and provide the types of qualitative data with which many managers and policymakers are most comfortable. Besides providing valid data on program performance and on problems inhibiting better performance, site visits present opportunities for testing new performance measures.

As tools for assessing program performance and results, however, on-site case studies suffer from five problems: (1) their tendency to overemphasize process and underemphasize program outcomes; (2) unreliability of measurement, because of variations among site visitors in the data they collect and in their interpretations of the data; (3) difficulties in generalizing to the entire program, because of limits on numbers of sites examined; (4) difficulties in completing site-visit reports; and (5) difficulties in communicating what was learned from the site visits. Fortunately, all of these problems can be dealt with. Service delivery assessments, for example, collect both process and short-term outcome data, cross-check findings from large numbers of sites, restrict the time within which reports are completed, and communicate their findings through twenty-minute briefings and reports limited to fifteen-twenty pages (see Chapter 6).

As vehicles for assessing program performance, on-site case studies suffer reliability and communication problems occasioned by the very richness of the data available. Observing different things at the same site or using different standards for judging performance, visitors may bring back different findings from the same site. And site-visit reports are difficult to complete. Voluminous data are often available on site; even conscientious site visitors often fail to complete their site-visit reports for considerable periods of time; and site-visit reports are difficult to summarize and absorb.

The evaluability assessment process (Chapters 2 and 3) provides a useful framework for efficient site visits and site-visit reporting. Evaluability assessment focuses the data collection on local progress in achieving specific results and on problems inhibiting better results; it also provides a convenient framework for summarizing site-visit findings. The second example in this chapter demonstrates the use of evaluability assessment as a framework for efficient conduct, completion, and communication of on-site case studies.

## Sampling

It will usually be too costly to collect data from all sites and from all those served by a program. To minimize data collection costs, sampling is usually necessary. Random sampling or stratified random sampling is often desirable, to ensure that the data collected are representative of the program in question. On the other hand, sampling may be done purposefully in order to reduce costs or to ensure that best practices are documented.

Random sampling of respondents or sites (by tossing coins or using tables of random numbers) reduces the number of respondents from whom data must be collected to get reliable estimates of program performance, while making it possible to generalize with known confidence to the universe from which the random sample was selected. Stratified random sampling (random sampling of groups of respondents and subsampling within groups) provides information on performance variations among groups, and allows more efficient sampling by making it possible to take advantage of smaller within-group performance variations.

In approaching the problem of efficient sampling in collecting program performance data, I have found two rules extremely helpful:

— The "square-root law": At a given confidence level, the precision of an estimate based on sample data varies with the square root of the number of respondents contacted.[6] (To estimate the proportion of women who have received adequate prenatal care, for example, a randomly selected sample of only twenty-five would almost always yield an estimate within 20 percent of the true value. A sample of one hundred would almost always yield an estimate within 10 percent of the true value; a sample of four hundred would almost always yield an estimate within 5 percent of the true value.) Fairly small samples can therefore be used in making rough estimates of program accomplishments.

— "Wholey's law": Consult an expert! Collection of survey data or site-visit data is usually the greatest part of the cost of an evaluation. Efficient sampling can save many hours and many dollars. I have found it well worth while to consult a survey research center in deciding on sample designs and sample sizes. The experts might point out, for example, that it is unnecessary to operate at the 95 percent confidence level. By instead operating at the 90 percent confidence level, which will be sufficient in many practical situations, the evaluator may be able to reduce data collection costs by 20 percent.

## Strengths and Weaknesses of Data Collection Options

In collecting data on program performance, a variety of data collection methods will normally be used.

Agency records and existing data series are sometimes used to minimize data collection costs. Program reporting systems and mail questionnaires are often used to obtain new data at minimal cost.

To ensure data validity and minimize perceived burden on respondents, a combination of telephone surveys and site visits will often be more appropriate than reliance on reports from the field. In the federal government in the 1980s, for example, when efforts are being made to reduce reporting burdens, evaluators will often have to rely primarily on telephone surveys and site visits. Examples 1 and 2 later in this chapter present a powerful, fairly inexpensive system for assessing program performance while imposing only light burdens on local sites.

# EVALUATION DESIGN OPTIONS

In addition to specification of program performance indicators, data sources, and data collection methods, development of a system for assessing program performance requires decisions on the comparisons to be made. Three important types of comparisons are available: (1) nonexperimental evaluation designs, (2) quasi-experimental designs, and (3) (randomized) experimental designs. Nonexperimental designs use only the data on program performance; randomized experiments and quasi-experiments also use comparison data to estimate the extent to which the program caused the observed results.

Contrary to many works on evaluation that direct policymakers, managers, and evaluators toward randomized experiments as the preferred option, this book focuses on management-oriented evaluation of ongoing programs. In ongoing programs it is usually impossible to use randomized experimental designs.

## Nonexperimental Designs

Nonexperimental evaluation designs use program performance data but do not use data on the performance of comparison groups. The most important nonexperimental designs are qualitative case studies and outcome monitoring systems.

Qualitative evaluations use in-depth, open-ended interviewing, personal observations, detailed descriptions, direct quotations, and excerpts from documents to gain understanding of individual cases before attempting generalizations. (See, for example, Michael Patton's excellent book, *Qualitative Evaluation Methods.*[7]) Qualitative evaluation methods are examined here in Chapters 2 and 3 (evaluability assessment), in Chapter 6 (service delivery assessment), and in Example 2 later in this chapter.

Outcome monitoring systems document program performance and intra-program variations in performance; they then compare program performance with prior or expected performance (see this chapter's Example 1 and Chapter 7). Outcome monitoring is similar to the monitoring done in management-by-objectives (MBO) systems and is therefore familiar to managers and policymakers. Outcome monitoring goes beyond typical MBO systems by focusing on program outcomes rather than on input or process objectives. If continued long enough, outcome monitoring systems can provide the time series data needed for quasi-experimental "interrupted time series" evaluations that estimate the effects of program changes by comparing trends in program outcomes before and after the program change.

## Quasi-experimental Designs

Quasi-experimental evaluation designs use program performance data and comparison data to estimate the extent to which program activities have caused observed results.[8] The best quasi-experimental designs are the single interrupted time series and multiple interrupted time series designs. Since it is usually impossible to find equivalent comparison groups not exposed to the program, time series data are usually required for correctly estimating the effects of program activities in the absence of a randomized experiment.

*Single interrupted time series designs* compare preprogram trends with postprogram trends on relevant performance measures. Such designs provide convincing evidence, for example, of the effects of charging for telephone calls for Directory Assistance and the effects of the establishment of the 55 mph speed limit. (Calls for "Information" dropped sharply when charges for such calls were imposed.[9] And, though it may not have saved much fuel, imposition of the 55 mph speed limit reduced traffic fatalities substantially.)

Use of the single interrupted time series design requires that a program be put into effect abruptly; otherwise, it may be impossible to separate the effects of the program from the effects of other changes in the environment.

*Multiple interrupted time series designs* also use data on trends in the performance of relevant comparison groups. Use of relevant comparison series provides greater confidence that changes in performance trends are due to the program and not to changes in the environment. Multiple interrupted time series designs provide convincing evidence, for example, that Connecticut's 1955 crackdown on speeding reduced traffic fatalities (neighboring states did not experience reduced traffic fatalities during the same time period), and that the British Breathalyzer requirement reduced traffic casualties on weekend nights (traffic casualties did not drop during commuting hours).[10]

## (Randomized) Experimental Designs

To gain conclusive evidence on the effectiveness of program activities, true experimental designs randomly assign individuals to alternative treatments. Random assignment ensures that, within known limits, the groups exposed to different treatments will be similar in all other respects (measured and unmeasured). If those exposed to one treatment perform better than those exposed to another treatment, then we can confidently assume that the differences in treatments caused the observed differences in results. The famous Manhattan Bail Bond experiment, for example, showed that pretrial detention resulted in the conviction and imprisonment of many people who would have been set free if they had been allowed to remain in the community while awaiting trial.[11]

## Strengths and Weaknesses of Alternative Evaluation Designs

Though qualitative case studies provide data considered relevant by managers and policymakers, they are costly and tend to be unreliable. Different observers may report different findings on the basis of open-ended interviews with the same respondents, examination of the same documents, or visits to the same sites.

Of the evaluation designs we have discussed, outcome monitoring tends to be the most feasible and the least expensive. It is also the least ambitious of the evaluation designs. Outcome monitoring does not attempt to determine whether the program caused observed changes in performance measures; instead, it allows managers and policymakers to make those judgments.

The single interrupted time series design requires a good deal of preprogram and postprogram trend data. If such data can be obtained (for example, by using existing time series data or by reconstructing the baseline data) and if the program has been implemented fairly quickly, the single interrupted time series design is an excellent method for estimating program effectiveness.

Mutliple interrupted time series designs provide even more convincing evidence, when preprogram and postprogram performance trends for relevant comparison groups are available. Interrupted time series designs may be appropriate when changes are introduced into programs already covered by appropriate outcome monitoring systems or other suitable data series. The main problem with interrupted time series designs is the requirement for many preprogram and many postprogram data points.

Randomized experiments tend to be difficult or impossible to implement in ongoing programs. They may be feasible, however, in demonstration programs designed to gain knowledge about the effectiveness of new practices. When feasible (as in the testing of new drugs or new surgical procedures), randomized experiments provide the most convincing evidence as to the effectiveness of program activities or program changes.

For evaluations of individual projects or ongoing programs, outcome monitoring or interrupted time series designs are likely to be the preferred choices, avoiding the often-fruitless attempts to get data on suitable comparison groups. Qualitative case studies can add useful information on how program results are achieved and on problems inhibiting better results.

In block grant programs and in the many categorical grant programs that allow substantial intra-program variation, the most useful evaluation design will often be a combination of outcome monitoring (Chapter 7) and qualitative case studies documenting how higher-performing projects are achieving better results (see Example 2 in this chapter). Service delivery assessments (Chapter 6) may provide helpful qualitative information on overall program performance and on intra-program variations in performance. If the program includes demonstration grant funds, then these evaluations of the overall program may be supplemented by experimental demonstration projects designed to test ways to achieve better results.

## RAPID-FEEDBACK EVALUATION: ORIGIN AND SIGNIFICANCE

Assessing program performance takes time, but managers and policymakers often cannot — or will not — wait. What can be done to get performance information "right quick"?

Through a process known as *rapid-feedback evaluation,* evaluators can provide managers and policymakers with two products: (1) a quick preliminary assessment of program performance in terms of agreed-on program objectives and performance indicators; and (2) designs for more valid, more reliable full-scale evaluation. By quickly providing policymakers and managers with a preliminary evaluation that presents new information but speaks frankly of its own limitations, evaluators can be responsive to immediate information needs, avoid the "quick and dirty" evaluations that often mislead, and lay the groundwork for useful longer-term evaluations. Given policy and management agreement on the types of evidence desired, rapid-feedback evaluation helps the evaluator to strengthen or amend that agreement by testing it with real data on program performance. The preliminary evaluation may fully meet policy and management information needs or (more likely) partially meet policy and management information needs and facilitate informed decisions on the scope and intended uses of additional data collection and analysis.

Like evaluability assessment, rapid-feedback evaluation is part of a "sequential purchase of information" strategy that breaks evaluation into a series of stages, each stage being initiated only when the likely usefulness of the new information outweighs the costs of acquiring it.[12]

Rapid-feedback evaluation resulted from the recognition of two conditions: (1) the tendency of evaluators to rush into the field without careful attention to the feasibility and likely usefulness of data collection; (2) the reality that evaluators still are usually too slow to meet managers' and policymakers' time schedules. The proposed solution was to combine a careful job of evaluation design (which would include development and testing of the performance measures to be used in a full-scale evaluation) with the collection of sufficient additional performance data to allow production of a preliminary evaluation during the design of a full-scale evaluation. In the *rapid-feedback evaluation,* existing data would be analyzed, estimates of program effectiveness would be collected from knowledgeable observers, performance measures would be developed and tested, and planned full-scale evaluations would be pilot-tested with data samples that are "small" but still large enough to allow preliminary estimates of program accomplishments.

The first test of rapid-feedback evaluation showed that rapid-feedback evaluation could meet both specifications, producing a quick, credible preliminary evaluation of the Department of Housing and Urban Development's Operation Breakthrough program and a design subsequently used for full-scale evaluation of that program.[13] Though the Department had originally requested only the development of a design for evaluation of Operation Breakthrough (a program intended to stimulate mass production of housing), it agreed to allow the evaluators to test the new rapid-feedback evaluation approach as part of the evaluation design process. The Operation Breakthrough rapid-feedback evaluation collected data from program records, a literature review, interviews with those knowledgeable about the housing industry, and visits to project sites. The evaluators developed models of program resources, activities, and intended outcomes; developed rough estimates of the parameters in the model; and formulated alternative evaluation designs for consideration by the Department. The rapid-feedback evaluation reached the following conclusions:

1. Many of the things which Operation Breakthrough intended to accomplish directly did indeed happen. These include:
   a. Housing units have been built and marketed as intended.
   b. A majority of states have adopted statewide building codes, and a number of code reciprocity agreements among the states have been made. . . .
2. Some of the intended accomplishments apparently did not occur. Among these are:
   a. State and local authorities, by and large, have not begun effective housing market aggregation activity.
   b. Savings and loan institutions have not significantly changed their involvement or interest in the financing of industrialized housing production.
   c. The program did not directly stimulate significant innovation in housing production technology.
3. Because of the program's design, it will be impossible, in practice, ever to tell anything definitive about its effects on the nation's housing production and related industries, or on the institutional and attitudinal constraints to the use of industrialized housing production methods. Available data do not demonstrate measurable effects to date, and comparison of the size of the program intervention with the size of the problem area shows that no such effects should have been expected by this time. Long-term impact will also not be determinable, since the

state of knowledge concerning housing market interactions will not allow distinguishing Operation Breakthrough effects from those of other important factors.[14]

The preliminary evaluation captured the attention of Department of Housing and Urban Development staff and facilitated decisions on the full-scale evaluation that the Department had promised to Congress.[15]


## THE RAPID-FEEDBACK EVALUATION PROCESS

Rapid-feedback evaluation synthesizes available information on program performance, develops and tests new performance measures, produces a preliminary evaluation of program performance, and develops alternative designs for full-scale evaluations. Rapid-feedback evaluation is a five-step process: (1) collection of existing data on program performance, (2) collection of new data on program performance, (3) preliminary evaluation, (4) development and analysis of alternative designs for full-scale evaluation, and (5) assisting policy and management decisions.


### Collection of Existing Data on Program Performance

Given policy and management agreement on the program performance indicators to be used in assessing program performance (as a result of evaluability assessment, for example), rapid-feedback evaluation begins by collecting existing data on program performance in terms of those performance indicators. Data sources may include agency records, program data systems, monitoring reports, or past research, evaluation, and audit reports. The agreed-on program performance indicators efficiently focus the review of existing data, since much of the data will not be relevant to the agreed-on performance indicators.


### Collection of New Data on Program Performance

Next, the evaluators collect limited amounts of new data on program performance, using the agreed-on program performance indicators to focus data collection activities. Data sources may include interviews with knowledgeable observers, telephone surveys of project staffs or of clients, and site visits to projects in the field. Appropriate comparison data may also be collected at this time.

The goal is a set of performance measures and comparisons that will provide valid, reliable, and relevant information, but still be cost-feasible.

## Preliminary Evaluation

Based on the data collected in the steps above, the evaluator now produces a preliminary evaluation of program performance in terms of the agreed-on program performance indicators. The preliminary evaluation represents the best available estimate of program accomplishments, together with statements of the degree of uncertainty in the estimate because of small samples or conflicting evidence.

## Development and Analysis of Alternative
## Designs for Full-Scale Evaluation

Contrary to typical "quick and dirty" evaluation efforts, the rapid feedback evaluation supplements the preliminary evaluation with statements of the degree of uncertainty in the preliminary assessment and statements of the time and effort required to get more conclusive information. At this point, the evaluator analyzes alternative designs for full-scale evaluation in terms of their feasibility, cost, likely conclusiveness, and likely utility.

Each full-scale evaluation design will specify the performance measurements to be taken, the comparisons to be made, the intended uses of the program performance information, the resources to be committed to the evaluation, and the work plan and schedule for the evaluation.

The analysis examines the strengths and weaknesses of: alternative performance measures (discussed earlier in this chapter), the costs of alternative sample sizes that could be used in estimating program performance or intra-program performance variations, and the strengths and weaknesses of nonexperimental, quasi-experimental, and experimental designs (also discussed earlier). The preferred alternatives for evaluation of ongoing programs will usually be qualitative case studies, comparisons of program performance with prior or expected performance, interrupted time series analyses, or some combination of these.

## Assisting Policy and Management Decisions

Rapid-feedback evaluation findings are presented in reports and briefings outlining the preliminary evaluation findings, the remaining uncertainties regarding program performance, options for immediate use of the preliminary evaluation data, and options for additional data collection and analysis.

Like all management-oriented evaluation, rapid-feedback evaluation is intended to assist policy and management decisions on program resources, program activities, program objectives, and collection and use of program performance information. Though the preliminary evaluation may be the occasion for decisions on program resources, activities, or objectives, the primary purpose of the rapid-feedback evaluation is to gain informed commitment to the conduct and future use of the planned full-scale evaluation.

As with the evaluability assessment options, presentation of the options for full-scale evaluation will involve managers and policymakers in decisions on the collection and intended use of program performance data. Because more time and effort have gone into collecting and analyzing program performance data, the evaluator can now be more precise about the costs of future data collection. The availability of real, rather than hypothetical, data also allows managers and policymakers to make more informed commitments to intended uses of any additional data collection.

In some cases, policymakers, managers, or evaluators may conclude that the rapid-feedback evaluation has provided sufficient information for substantive program or policy decisions; or they may conclude that additional data collection is unlikely to be sufficiently conclusive or useful to justify its cost. In these cases, the evaluation may stop with the rapid feedback, thus averting most of the cost of the originally planned full-scale evaluation.

## EXAMPLE 1: DEVELOPMENT AND TEST OF
## AN OUTCOME MONITORING SYSTEM
## BASED ON TELEPHONE SURVEYS

Evaluations of large programs are difficult, both because of the cost of data collection and because wide variations in local activities or objectives often complicate the task of collecting comparable data from different sites. The diversity at local level also makes it difficult to summarize what is being accomplished in a large program — a difficulty that strikes at the heart of the concepts of "results-oriented management" and "demonstrably effective programs."

For large programs three options are available: (1) to treat the large program as a "revenue sharing" program, the purpose of which is simply to transfer resources to another level of government; (2) to monitor the local sites in terms of a uniform set of program objectives and performance indicators; or (3) to develop a system for monitoring and reporting on the diversity of activities undertaken and results achieved at local level.

In Chapters 1–4 we usually wrote as if option 2 were the only feasible option for results-oriented managers. This and the following section show how results-oriented managers can pursue option 3 in a categorical program. Similar activities will be appropriate in many block grant programs.

In this and the following section, we examine a system developed to assess the performance and results of the Health Planning program, a federal program established to stimulate state and local planning and regulatory activities that would restrain rising health care costs and improve the health care system. In 1978, the time at which this outcome monitoring system was developed, the Health Planning program was administered by the Bureau of Health Planning, one of the bureaus in the U.S. Department of Health, Education, and Welfare (HEW).

Under a contract with HEW, the Urban Institute conducted two rapid-feedback evaluations focused on development and testing of a system for monitoring the performance and impact of local health systems agencies (HSAs).

Most monitoring systems rely on process data. Instead, the bureau's new monitoring system used telephone surveys of samples of HSAs and follow-up site visits to subsamples of HSAs to

Example 1    125

collect (1) information on results achieved (and results likely to be achieved) at the local level, and (2) case studies of programs that appeared likely to produce positive impacts on the local health care system.[16] The monitoring system was designed (1) to assess the performance of health systems agencies in producing realistic plans and in achieving local and national objectives for changes in the health care system, and (2) to document the processes through which health systems agencies solved specific problems and achieved specific types of changes in the health care system. Information from the monitoring system was to be used to report program accomplishments to Congress, to HEW, and to the Office of Management and Budget; to minimize negative effects of federal regulations and guidelines; and to increase the effectiveness of federal technical assistance activities and products.[17]

The first rapid-feedback evaluation pilot-tested the telephone survey portion of the planned impact monitoring system by developing and testing survey questionnaires and procedures. The telephone surveys had four goals: (1) to produce valid data at low cost; (2) to be relevant to Bureau of Health Planning managers' specific information needs; (3) to be easily adjusted to meet changes in information requirements; and (4) to produce information more quickly than typical monitoring systems.[18] Bureau managers triggered the monitoring process by defining topic areas to be monitored (for example, supply and utilization of general hospital beds). In four surveys, a total of twenty-nine health systems agencies provided information on fifteen health planning topic areas, though not all of the HSAs were questioned about each topic. In the surveys, questions were asked as to whether the HSAs had adopted local standards for changes in the health care system related to national objectives; whether they had systems for assessing local performance in terms of the local standards; whether they used the local standards in reviewing proposed changes in the health care system; whether they had completed the design of local programs likely to achieve the local standards by 1984; and whether they planned to measure resulting changes in health care costs. Based on the four surveys, the rapid feedback evaluation came to the following conclusions:

— Most HSAs, 73–86 percent, reported adopting standards for general hospital beds, obstetrical services, and CT scanners.
— Approximately half of the HSAs, 40–55 percent, reported adopting stan-

dards in pediatric services, radiation therapy, neonatal intensive care, cardiology, and HMOs.

— About one-half of the HSAs that reported adopting a standard for a cost containment related planning area also reported a completed program design for achieving the standard. For example, 86 percent of the HSAs reported adopting a standard for general hospital beds, but only 41 percent reported a completed program design.[19]

For specific cost-containment areas, information from the telephone surveys was summarized in terms of criteria akin to those that characterize results-oriented management:

— establishment of local standards for changes in the health care system
— existence of a system for assessing local performance in terms of the standard
— design of a program to achieve the standard by 1984
— likelihood of achievement of the local standard by 1984 rated medium or high
— existence of a system for measuring resulting changes in health care costs.[20]

The rapid-feedback evaluation had this conclusion:

The tentative findings from the telephone surveys indicate that the HSAs have established the foundation required to develop fully programs that affect . . . local health care systems consistent with national priorities.[21]

Since most health systems agencies had set standards related to supply and utilization of general hospital beds, the rapid-feedback evaluation went on to recommend priorities for results-oriented management by the bureau in this area:

— Closely monitor actual impact of leading HSA programs to assure that their efforts are consistent with Bureau policies.
— Tailor technical assistance and Bureau directives to move as many HSAs in the direction of the most developed programs. . . .

Specifically, Bureau attention might best be focused on fostering institution-specific recommendations for changes in local health care systems. As we see it, there is no way to actually alter the configuration of the health care system without being specific about which institutions need to change and exactly why the change is necessary. Some HSAs have already developed this "implementation" function to quite a high level.[22]

Example 1    127

The report also contained an important policy recommendation:

[In] the areas selected by Bureau managers as priorities for cost containment, the telephone survey data indicate that HSAs concentrate in the areas of general hospital beds, obstetrical services, and CT scanners. This information could be used by the Bureau to help cut back the large number of specific objectives defined by most HSAs. This might be a tangible step toward resolving the problem of dissipated HSA resources.[23]

The rapid-feedback evaluation concluded with findings on the feasibility and cost of the telephone surveys. From the point of view of those interested in results-oriented management, the report identified an important problem:

— Although the majority of HSAs seemed to support the need for impact monitoring, the most pronounced responses came from about 28 percent, who registered negative reactions to the specific survey instrument they received. For the most part, these reactions seem to imply that the HSAs are afraid that their efforts will be misrepresented or misconstrued. Given the nature of the questions, which drive hard at bottom-line concerns (like when can the HSA's program be expected to produce demonstrable results), this form of misgiving could be expected regardless of the form of the questioning. In the future, the delicate operation of administering telephone surveys for monitoring HSA impact might continue to be conditioned by the fact that questions about potential to affect the local health care system follow years of process-oriented directives to local health planning agencies.[24]

Costs of the telephone surveys were presented as follows:

Including Bureau and Institute staff, the entire . . . effort on the prototype telephone survey required an estimated 50-55 professional person-days. . . . The amount of . . . staff time spent administering a survey to an individual HSA was about three hours. This included contacting the HSA, recoding the HSA's responses, and offloading the collected data for presentation to the policy group.

The cost to the HSAs is estimated to be about three hours of time per survey when time spent preparing to respond to the questionnaire is included.[25]

The rapid feedback evaluation concluded that the test of the prototype telephone surveys was successful, noting that the bureau had judged that the telephone surveys provided useful information, had decided to continue the use of telephone surveys for HSA impact monitoring, and had begun to develop surveys for state agency impact monitoring.

Because of the diversity of national and local health planning objectives, the type of monitoring system developed for the Health Planning program has broad implications for federal and state programs. What was developed for the Health Planning program is an example of the type of monitoring systems appropriate in a large categorical grant program, when managers and policymakers wish to determine whether program goals and objectives are being taken seriously at local level and to determine the program's potential for effective performance. In addition, this type of monitoring system is suitable for getting information on state and local accomplishments in block grant programs. This information could be used in national or state leadership of activities conducted in the block grant program. It could also be used at budget time or at the time of legislative reauthorization, when the value of a block grant program is likely to be questioned.

## EXAMPLE 2: DEVELOPMENT AND TEST OF A QUALITATIVE EVALUATION SYSTEM BASED ON EVALUABILITY-ASSESSMENT CASE STUDIES OF LOCAL PROGRAMS

As mentioned above, case studies are an attractive but problematic method for assessing program performance. This section presents a method for conducting case studies that avoids many of the problems identified in the section "Evaluation Design Options" and efficiently produces relevant, reliable information.

The second rapid-feedback evaluation of the Health Planning program used a scaled-down version of the evaluability assessment methodology to produce case studies of health systems agency (HSA) programs that appeared to have high potential for influencing the health care system. These programs were identified through the telephone surveys described in the preceding section.

The case studies were to be used to verify findings from the telephone surveys and to document examples of good local practices. The examples were to be used in development of federal regulations and guidelines and in development of technical assistance products likely to be effectively used by other health systems agencies. The case studies would include, for example,

Example 2   129

estimates of the calendar time and staff-time required for health systems agencies to produce specific changes in the local health care system.[26]

Information on promising local programs was collected using the evaluability assessment approach to document individual HSA programs. The case-study approach included (1) a description of the local program in terms of a sequence of events identifying the resources, activities, and intended accomplishments of the local program; (2) descriptions of the events; (3) measures and comparisons defining the events; (4) descriptions of the activities necessary for each event to occur; (5) descriptions of the information systems providing evidence that the events had occurred; and (6) descriptions of intended HSA uses of information on local program performance and results.[27]

The case studies were completed using the evaluability assessment methodology. Data were collected from HSA plans available at federal level; through telephone surveys; and through interviews with key health systems agency managers, observations of HSA activities, and reviews of information available at the local sites. The evaluators used the data in judging whether the local programs were likely to achieve their objectives.[28]

The rapid-feedback evaluation report described this qualitative evaluation system, illustrated it with findings from three prototype on-site studies, and presented a full illustration of the findings from one of the three health systems agencies visited.

The rapid-feedback evaluation noted that the site visits confirmed the validity of the data obtained from the telephone surveys.[29] The site visits also provided important information not obtained from the telephone surveys:

> The site visits added immeasurably to the design group's ability to interpret survey findings. For example, on site it was possible to probe the relationship between the HSA and local hospitals in much more depth than the telephone surveys could. . . .
> A precondition to actually making changes in the health care system seems to be HSA objectives for the institutional level. . . .
> With the understanding gained on site about levels of objectives, we were able to tighten our criteria for assessing potential for impact for HSA programs. All other things being equal, an HSA with institution-specific objectives that coordinated with an areawide objective was judged to have a higher potential for achieving an actual impact than an HSA with only an areawide

standard. Telephone surveys are expected in the future to concentrate much more specifically on this "level of objectives" aspect of HSA health planning initiatives.[30]

The bulk of the rapid-feedback evaluation report consisted of a thirty-page case study of an effective southeastern Wisconsin HSA program, "Regional Consolidation of Obstetrical Services," and nineteen pages of appendices listing the fifty-three HSA documents reviewed and presenting the HSA's policies and procedures for implementation planning. Excerpts from this case study are presented to illustrate the power of the technique:

### II. OVERVIEW OF SOUTHEASTERN WISCONSIN'S PROGRAM FOR OBSTETRICAL SERVICES

This chapter briefly describes the situation or setting of the on-site case study. Included in this discussion are vital characteristics of the HSA, dimensions of the problem . . . , an outline of the structure of the program, "regional consolidation of obstetrical services," a brief summary of the program's impact so far on the local health care system, and some findings about the cost of the program. Impact is expressed in terms of obstetrical unit closures and consolidations and institutional cost savings.

#### A. The Health Systems Agency

The Southeastern Wisconsin Health Systems Agency, Inc., is a large, well organized agency serving about 1,781,000 residents of the seven counties in and around Milwaukee. For the year starting in May 1977, the total direct cost of operating the HSA was $924,016. Ninety-two percent of these funds were received from the Public Health Service, while local county governments and the United Ways contributed the remainder.

The agency has a staff of 44 in four main divisions, Planning and Research, Health System Development, Review, and Communications. . . .

#### B. The Problem

Consolidating regional obstetrical services can solve the problem of misallocated regional obstetrical care resources. In this instance, more maternity beds, delivery rooms, bassinets, nurses, etc., were available than were needed. The HSA cited occupancy rates for obstetrical units and delivery rates to demonstrate the extent of the problem. According to the telephone survey that preceded the site visit, the average annual occupancy rate for obstetrics in SEW was 60.7 percent. This underutilization resulted in an 11 to 39 percent oversupply of beds, depending on the method of need analysis employed.

An oversupply of obstetrical resources is waste that inflates the cost of

Example 2    131

providing obstetric services. According to a 1976 survey of 6,187 households in Southeastern Wisconsin, 62 percent term the cost of health care "excessive." . . . Not surprisingly, a central expectation for consolidation is cost containment. . . .

In 1976, there were 28 institutions providing obstetric services [in Southeastern Wisconsin] . . . . Considering that the minimum recommended number of deliveries per year is 1,500 for most of the hospitals, the data show clearly that the area is oversupplied with obstetric resources. There are allowances, however, for low delivery rates in areas where access is difficult. For example, the low delivery rates for the two obstetric units in the southwest subarea are acceptable, because the units serve separate, somewhat isolated populations.

## C. Program to Address the Problem

The SEWHSA's program for consolidating regional obstetric and perinatal services depends on arriving at a series of successively more specific agreements on the best way to modify the current configuration of facilities and services to enhance overall birth-related care in the area. For the most part the HSA staff acts as a facilitator, researcher, and broker in this process, while the HSA board, the community, and the providers work out the terms of each agreement with the hospitals that control facilities and service units.

The move to consolidate facilities and services started with an agreement by the HSA board to invest HSA staff resources on a "special study" of obstetric and perinatal services. Based on the study findings, review and revision from a technical advisory committee of physicians, and review and comment by the community and providers, the HSA board adopted specific guidelines for service for each of nine subareas and the entire region served by the HSA.

Another round of HSA staff studies was necessary to determine how best to consolidate obstetric resources to meet the new guidelines. This process, which produced an "implementation plan" with recommendations for institution-specific or community-specific changes in facilities and services, again involved the community and providers. Of course, this special study and implementation plan are also linked to the HSA's Health Systems Plan and Annual Implementation Plan under PL 93–641 and the HSA's annual recommendation to the State Health Planning and Resource Development Agency. . . .

Next, the HSA staff met and negotiated with hospitals that would be affected by the recommendations. At this stage, the HSA staff conducted a study on cost tradeoffs at the institutional level for service consolidation. To date, six hospitals have formally agreed to the recommendations. These are perhaps the most critical agreements in the program — those that actually change the configuration of area facilities and services.

In the future, more agreements are expected. In fact, the HSA staff expects to see a dynamic health care system with ever-changing service offerings and ever-changing ideas about how to administer health care most effectively.

### D. Impact on the Health Care System

Since 1976, the number of hospitals providing obstetric services in southeastern Wisconsin has dropped by 10 percent. Another 10 percent reduction is expected within the next two years. By late 1980, SEWHSA expects to be about halfway to its objective, which is to reduce the number of operating obstetric and perinatal service units from 28 to 19. In the early 1980's this goal should be achieved. Each obstetrical service unit closure has caused a net reduction in total obstetric beds in the subarea served by the closed service unit.

### E. Cost of the Program

Regional consolidation of obstetric services has been a major area of planning for the Southeastern Wisconsin HSA since the early 1970's. Therefore, the overall cost of the program is probably a significant portion of the HSA's staff investment over the years compared to the costs of other specific planning areas. For example, there have been at least seven studies associated with the program, numerous HSA board level meetings, and many meetings with local hospital administrators and other representatives of both providers and the community. . . .

The cost of the program is high. Few separate efforts such as the obstetrics consolidation could be undertaken simultaneously given its cost. Therefore, SEWHSA is trying to find ways to cut the cost. One suggestion is to combine the special study and implementation study parts of the program.

### III. DESCRIPTION OF THE PROGRAM

#### A. Overview

The following section presents the main elements of the program as described by the HSA staff. The description is summarized [in Figure 5-1], a simple model that organizes main events or phases in consolidating obstetric services. . . .

#### B. Strategy for Change

*1. Event I*

The first event in SEWHSA's program was a "special study" of current capacity and future need for birth-related services conducted by HSA staff using established health planning methods. This involved determining the current status of the area as a whole and of each of the subareas in relation to about 75 factors. . . .

*2. Event II*

The second event uses information on current status and findings from analyses developed by the HSA staff during event I. A technical advisory committee composed of obstetricians reviewed the staff's findings and made basic recommendations to a regional planning standing committee. . . .

Example 2    133

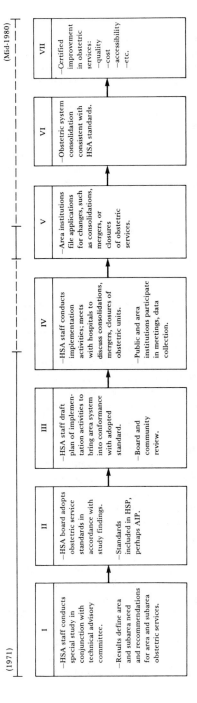

**Figure 5-1 Southeastern Wisconsin HSA Program for Regional Consolidation of Obstetrical Services: Event Sequence and Event Descriptions** (*Source:* James B. Bell, *Rapid Feedback Evaluation Report Two: Prototype On-Site Case Studies of HSA Programs* (Washington, D.C.: The Urban Institute, 1978), p. 24.)

### 3. Event III

During event III, HSA staff and board concentrated on how to realign birth-related services in the region. The result was subarea and institution-specific recommendations, formulated with community and provider participation. Specifically, the main thrust of activities during the event was to develop an "implementation plan," which was defined as "a process which proposes the future role of facilities which are capable, or potentially capable, of delivering the service or services under consideration. . . ."

The process for making these recommendations involved the HSA board and staff and the community in about 12 separate activities. The process was expected to last 120 days but was significantly disrupted when one community objected vociferously to a recommendation that would affect its local hospital. Nearly 20,000 people registered discontent with the recommendation in the implementation plan until they were informed that it was a draft for public comment and not an edict from the HSA. This community calmly accepted the same consolidation scheme . . . when it was actually put into effect. . . .

### 4. Event IV

The objective of event IV is to realize the consolidations, mergers, and obstetric unit closures expressed in the plan for implementation. Meetings with hospital administrators and their representatives are necessary to reach agreements about which service units should be merged or closed. . . .

Part of the process of implementing recommendations was another study phase. A supplement report, prepared by the Health System Development Division staff with data provided by the hospital, focused on the advantages and disadvantages of trading obstetrics for pediatrics in the Kenosha/St. Catherine's consolidation and examines cost tradeoffs for the hospitals. . . .

HSA staff point out the importance of event IV activities in terms of health care resources. For example, they report that meetings between HSA staff and representatives of Lutheran Hospital and Columbia Hospital have expanded to include representatives of a neighboring hospital. As a result, the scope of the negotiations has been expanded. Meetings that were originally intended to achieve a merger of obstetric services in two hospitals now may result in consolidation of three entire hospitals into only two.

### 5. Event V

Event V is expected to result in review decisions by the HSA consistent with agreements reached during event IV. This is where the SEWHSA's considerable facilities and program review authority came into play. Once an agreement is reached through the planning activities and negotiations outlined above, the review itself is essentially pro forma. Until that time, the review process is the main leverage available to the HSA for gaining agreement between institutions. Without review, it would be much more difficult to bring regional obstetrical resources into compliance with standards set by the

Example 2   135

HSA. Thus, the review process plays a quiet but powerful role in the program. . . .

### 6. Event VI

Event VI activities occur within the region's hospitals and involve the actual reconfiguration of obstetric and perinatal service units to conform with area guidelines, implementation plan and supplemental report findings and recommendations, and certificate of need application decisions.

During this phase, institutions that have agreed to modify obstetric services implement their commitments. Although these actions occur inside the hospitals (outside the purview of the general public and the HSA but with public accountability through the HSA planning process), they are critical to the overall consolidation efforts. The whole program is just an expensive paper process unless the number of delivery rooms, bassinets, short-stay maternity recovery beds, and so on is changed to conform with the guidelines adopted during the first phase of the program.

When this happens the health care system will be demonstrably changed, and the last phase of the program begins.

### 7. Event VII

Event VII consists of measurement and analysis activities. SEWHSA expects to demonstrate that obstetric service costs at participating institutions are more contained than the costs at uncontrolled hospital service cost centers.

Event VII assesses the net result of the agreements that lead to system change. Changing the regional health care system is expected to lead to improved individual care and contained costs for individual obstetric patients. The SEWHSA's consolidation program for obstetric services is weakest in this area. . . .

### C. CONCLUSION

The SEWHSA's program for consolidation of regional obstetric services seems particularly well developed in events I through V. . . .

The program is less well developed for event VI, which involves hospitals changing service offerings, facilities, staff assignment, equipment, supplies, etc., and event VII, HSA evaluation of the overall program achievements. In essence, a number of questions will have to be answered in order to substantiate what seems to be a very high potential for achievement. . . .[31]

Based on the site visits conducted in the rapid-feedback evaluation, the evaluators estimated the evaluation system costs to be approximately fifteen to twenty professional staff days per site (approximately one day to prepare for the site visit, several staff days for on-site activities, including one day to verify the content of the report with the local health systems agency, and several staff days for writing the case study report) and five to seven secretarial days per site.[32]

When presented with the prototype site-visit reports, Bureau of Health Planning managers reacted very favorably. They immediately initiated a new series of site visits to gather data that could be used in reporting Health Planning program status to high-level HEW officials and to Congress. They followed up by implementing an HSA impact monitoring system based on use of the telephone surveys and on-site case studies.[33]

## CONCLUSION

Rapid-feedback evaluations test the feasibility and cost of specific performance measures, and they produce preliminary evaluations in terms of a framework of agreed-on program objectives and performance indicators. In some cases, the preliminary evaluation will be sufficient for policy and management action; in other cases, the rapid-feedback evaluation will provide a good foundation for subsequent full-scale evaluation.

In the next chapter we turn to a somewhat similar evaluation process, service delivery assessment, which can play similar roles even in the absence of agreement on program objectives and performance indicators.

## NOTES TO CHAPTER 5

1. James Bell provided helpful comments on an earlier draft of this chapter.

2. John W. Scanlon, "Developing Performance Measures" (Lecture at the University of Southern California's Washington Public Affairs Center, Washington, D.C., November 23, 1980).

3. See, for example, Alfred J. Tuchfarber and William R. Klecka, *Random Digit Dialing: Lowering the Cost of Victimization Surveys* (Washington, D.C.: Police Foundation, 1976).

4. See Joseph R. Hochstim, "A Critical Comparison of Three Strategies of Collecting Data from Households, "*American Statistical Association Journal,* vol. 62, no. 319 (September 1967), pp. 976–989; and Alfred J. Tuchfarber and others, "Reducing the Cost of Victim Surveys," in Wesley C. Skogan, ed., *Sample Surveys of the Victims of Crime* (Cambridge, Mass.: Ballinger Books, 1976).

5. See, for example, Alfred H. Schainblatt and Harry P. Hatry, *Mental Health Services: What Happens to the Clients?* (Washington, D.C.: The Urban Institute, 1979).

6. Henry W. Riecken and Robert F. Boruch, eds., *Social Experimentation: A Method for Planning and Evaluating Social Intervention* (New York: Academic Press, 1974), p. 71.

7. Michael Quinn Patton, *Qualitative Evaluation Methods* (Beverly Hills, Calif.: Sage Publications, 1980).

8. See Thomas D. Cook and Donald T. Campbell, *Quasi-Experimentation: Design and Analysis Issues for Field Settings* (Chicago: Rand McNally College Publishing Company, 1979); Stephen Isaac and William B. Michael, *Handbook in Research and Evaluation*, 2d ed. (San Diego, Calif.: EdITS Publishers, 1981); and Eugene Stone, *Research Methods in Organizational Behavior* (Glenview, Ill.: Scott, Foresman, 1978).

9. Cook and Campbell, *Quasi-Experimentation*, pp. 270-271.

10. Riecken and Boruch, *Social Experimentation*, pp. 101-103.

11. See Bernard Botein, "The Manhattan Bail Project: Its Impact on Criminology and the Criminal Law Processes," *Texas Law Review*, vol. 43 (1965), pp. 319-331; and Herbert Sturz, "Experiments in the Criminal Justice System," *Legal Aid Briefcase*, February 1967, pp. 111-115.

12. See Joseph S. Wholey, *Evaluation: Promise and Performance* (Washington, D.C.: The Urban Institute, 1979).

13. See Donald R. Weidman, Francine L. Tolson, and Joseph S. Wholey, *Summary of Initial Assessment and Evaluation Study Design for Operation Breakthrough*, Report prepared for the Department of Housing and Urban Development (Washington, D.C.: The Urban Institute, 1974); Donald R. Weidman, *An Example of Rapid Feedback Evaluation: The Operation Breakthrough Experience* (Washington, D.C.: The Urban Institute, 1976); and Wholey, *Evaluation: Promise and Performance*, pp. 89-90.

14. Weidman, Tolson, and Wholey, *Summary of Initial Assessment*, pp. 7-8.

15. Donald R. Weidman, "Operation Breakthrough," Evaluation Seminar, Office of the Assistant Secretary for Planning and Evaluation, U.S. Department of Health, Education, and Welfare, Washington, D.C., March 8, 1979.

16. James B. Bell, *Rapid Feedback Evaluation Report One: Prototype Telephone Surveys for HSA Impact Monitoring*, Report prepared under Department of Health, Education, and Welfare Contract No. HEW-100-77-0028 (Washington, D.C.: The Urban Institute, 1978), p. iii.

17. Ibid., p. 10.

18. Ibid., pp. 11-12.

19. Ibid., pp. 29-30.

20. Ibid., p. 35. (See the results-oriented management scale suggested in Chapter 1, Table 1-1.)

21. Ibid., p. 41.

22. Ibid., p. 42.

23. Ibid., p. 45.

24. Ibid., p. 43.

25. Ibid., pp. 43–44.

26. James B. Bell, *Rapid Feedback Evaluation Report Two: Prototype On-Site Case Studies of HSA Programs*, Report prepared under Department of Health, Education, and Welfare Contract No. HEW–100–77–0028 (Washington, D.C.: The Urban Institute, 1978), p. 2.

27. Ibid., p. 3.

28. The local evaluability assessments were "scaled-down versions" of the methodology presented in Richard E. Schmidt, John W. Scanlon, and James B. Bell, *Evaluability Assessment: Making Public Programs Work Better* (Rockville, Md.: U.S. Department of Health, Education, and Welfare, Project Share, Human Services Monograph No. 14, 1979). See Chapters 2 and 3.

29. Bell, *Rapid Feedback Evaluation Report Two*, p. 9.

30. Ibid., pp. 9–10.

31. Ibid., pp. 14–43.

32. Ibid., p. 13.

33. Ibid., p. 9.

# 6

## Service Delivery Assessment: A Goal-Free Evaluation Process

### INTRODUCTION

The evaluation approaches examined thus far have all been goal-oriented, directed at the identification of agreed-on program objectives and performance indicators, and at the evaluation of program performance in terms of the agreed-on objectives and indicators. In program evaluation, however, tunnel vision is always a concern. Important program outcomes may be missed if the evaluator's focus is too narrow. The evaluability assessment approach (Chapters 2–4) attempts to minimize the likelihood that important outcomes will be left out when the program objectives and performance indicators are identified. Still, evaluability assessment clearly is in the goal-oriented evaluation tradition: Subsequent rapid-feedback evaluation or full-scale evaluation would be done in terms of a set of objectives and performance indicators identified as a result of the evaluability assessment.

Here we examine a goal-free evaluation approach, in which evaluators attempt to document important program outcomes without the constraints imposed by a predetermined set of objectives and performance indicators. A goal-free evaluation approach can be especially useful if it is used as a quick preliminary probe, designed to ensure that the most important types of program outcomes are included in subsequent full-scale evaluation activities.

Service delivery assessment is an exciting new evaluation approach that provides top managers with current qualitative infor-

139

mation on the experiences and perceptions of large numbers of program clients and local service providers. Like investigative reporting, service delivery assessment (SDA) is a qualitative evaluation process that collects information through open-ended interviews with clients, local service providers, and program officials. In an average of three to five months from start to finish, service delivery assessment provides information on program activities, information on those served and on those needing services, and information on problems in service delivery. Like the rapid-feedback evaluation approach described in Chapter 5, service delivery assessment produces a preliminary evaluation of program performance that either may be sufficient for policy or management action or may lead to more definitive full-scale evaluation.

Invented by top federal policymakers and managers who needed to know more about the programs for which they were responsible, service delivery assessment has proven to be a form of evaluation that meets policymakers' and managers' information needs. It contributes to improved understanding, better policy and management decisions, and better-targeted ongoing data collection. Though not the answer in every situation, service delivery assessment can be very helpful when policymakers or managers need clearer perceptions of program reality or early warning of emerging problems.

This chapter describes the origin of service delivery assessment, the service delivery assessment process, management uses of service delivery assessment findings, and the organization and management of the service delivery assessment program. An example is included to illustrate service delivery assessment products and uses.[1]

## ORIGIN OF SERVICE DELIVERY ASSESSMENT

Early in their careers in the Department of Health, Education, and Welfare (HEW), Secretary Joseph A. Califano, Jr., and Under Secretary Hale Champion created a new evaluation system that would provide them with immediate feedback on program operations. As part of a departmental reorganization, Califano and Champion changed the former regional Planning and Evaluation staffs into

Offices of Service Delivery Assessment in each of the ten HEW regional offices. These offices reported to the Principal Regional Officials but were under the functional management of HEW Inspector General Thomas D. Morris, who was a trusted adviser to Secretary Califano.

Wanting direct feedback from the operation of HEW programs but impatient with the relatively slow pace of evaluation research studies, Califano and Champion created a new evaluation tool that allowed them to bypass bureaucratic and intergovernmental layers and get firsthand information from people directly involved in service delivery. As the Secretary's "eyes and ears," the service delivery assessment staffs were directed to produce quick (three- to five-month) assessments on programs and issues personally selected by the Secretary and the Under Secretary.

Topics for service delivery assessments were (and are) selected by the Secretary or Under Secretary; the service delivery assessment teams briefed their findings directly to the Secretary or Under Secretary and other top managers in the department. Beginning with Head Start, one of Califano's favorite programs, service delivery assessment teams (in-house staff, not contractors) completed nine service delivery assessments in fiscal year 1978, sixteen in fiscal year 1979, and fourteen in fiscal year 1980. Following a pause occasioned by the transition to a new administration in 1981, new topics were selected for service delivery assessment in fiscal year 1981 and subsequent years.[2]

## THE SERVICE DELIVERY ASSESSMENT PROCESS

Little has yet been published on service delivery assessment. The following description of the service delivery assessment (SDA) process is based on publications by Michael Hendricks of the Office of Service Delivery Assessment in the U.S. Department of Health and Human Services (HHS) and on my own observations as an adviser to the service delivery assessment program.[3]

Service delivery assessments, typically conducted by staff from three to five of the HHS regional offices, are completed in three to five months. The service delivery assessment process consists of these five steps: (1) preassessment, (2) design, (3) data collection, (4) analysis of data, and (5) presentation of findings and recommendations.

### Preassessment (Four to Six Weeks)

In the preassessment phase, SDA staff visit several local sites; hold discussions with local, state, and federal program staff; complete a brief review of program legislation, regulations, past studies, and relevant data; and hold discussions with policy, budget, and evaluation staff and outside experts. The preassessment serves some of but not all the purposes of an evaluability assessment: Because it does not include interaction between evaluators and the Secretary, the preassessment does not and cannot achieve full closure on the Secretary's program objectives and information priorities.

Service delivery assessments are typically initiated when problems are suspected or policy changes are planned, or when the Secretary is interested in a particular program or issue. In the preassessment, SDA staff attempt to determine what the Secretary needs to learn and can learn from a relatively brief but fairly extensive look at field operations. The preassessment moves the service delivery assessment from a fairly general one-page assignment to decisions on the set of issues and questions to be addressed in the assessment.

### Design of the Service Delivery Assessment

In the design phase, SDA staff from the lead region specify the purpose of the assessment, the issues and questions to be addressed, the issues not to be addressed, and the study design: types of data to be collected, types and numbers of respondents to be interviewed, types and numbers of sites to be visited, types of data analyses to be done, the schedule for the assessment, and numbers and types of staff to be included in the assessment team.

The SDAs typically collect data from several hundred respondents in a total of fifteen to thirty sites, in six to ten states drawn from three to five of the ten HHS regions. Approximately 50 percent of the respondents are clients; 25 percent, local providers; and 25 percent, others (for example, people from advocacy groups, professional organizations, and local, state, and federal program staffs).

Sites to be visited are usually selected by purposeful sampling, though random sampling is sometimes used. Respondents are selected by purposeful or random sampling. (A number of observers have remarked that random sampling, at least in selection of the respondents to be interviewed, would allow both the SDA teams and decision makers to place more confidence in the SDA findings. Though decision makers have apparently not been troubled by the niceties of sampling strategy, the HHS Office of Service Delivery Assessment has begun to place greater stress on random sampling.)

Though the primary method of data collection has been face-to-face interviews, SDAs have increasingly been using telephone interviews as well. The SDA data collection instruments, normally discussion guides predominantly composed of open-ended questions, have in many cases been supplemented by on-site observation, use of photography, or analyses of case records and other program documents.

Once the evaluation design and the discussion guides have been completed, a major remaining task is to train all service delivery assessment team members on the data collection and analysis to be done. SDAs typically are conducted by a total of eight to sixteen regional office staff members. Early service delivery assessments used larger data collection teams including regional office staff detailed to the SDA team for several weeks; more recent SDAs have tended to use teams predominantly composed of full-time SDA staff. Training is preferably done by assembling the entire team at the lead region for two or three days, though limitations on resources may suggest a less costly training method. When only full-time SDA staff are used and the entire SDA team has been involved in the preassessment and design steps, the need for training may be reduced.

## Data Collection (Two to Three Weeks)

In the data collection phase, small teams of HHS regional staff spend three to five days at each of fifteen to thirty local sites, visiting day-care centers, health clinics, senior centers, nursing homes, welfare offices, and so on, and interviewing clients, providers, and others as appropriate.

The SDA data collection has been done principally through open-ended personal interviews, though SDA teams have increasingly been using telephone interviews as a supplementary data collection technique. As the SDA *Training Manual* notes about telephone interviews: "Speed and supervision are both improved. . . . In addition, the relative anonymity of telephoning . . . can sometimes lead to very frank discussions of the issues."[4]

Discussions are usually limited to thirty to forty-five minutes for client interviews and no more than sixty minutes for other respondents, with telephone interviews limited to approximately thirty minutes. Responses to open-ended questions are recorded "as nearly verbatim as possible."[5]

Group interviews, analyses of case records and other program documents, and photography have also been used to collect SDA data.

## Analysis of Data (Five to Six Weeks for Analysis and Report Writing)

Analyses of SDA data result in descriptions of local operations and local environments, comparisons among local sites, comparisons with standards of expected performance, early warnings of emerging problems, descriptions of best practices observed, and recommendations for operational improvements.

Because SDAs are done by teams from a number of HHS regional offices, SDA data are analyzed by three methods: (1) preparation of regional reports, including descriptive data, unexpected findings, team member perceptions, and quotes or examples to illustrate the findings; (2) a two- to three-day debriefing session, for regional team leaders and all SDA staff from the lead region, that provides the occasion for discussions of major findings, conclusions, and recommendations; and (3) analyses of the responses from all the individual interviews, often using after-the-fact coding of the responses to open-ended questions.

SDA reports often include illustrative quotes or case studies describing the experiences and attitudes of clients. The Foster Care SDA, for example, began with a preface composed of excerpts from an interview with a twenty-year-old girl who had lived in six foster homes between the ages of eight and eighteen. I found her message personally challenging:

I needed attention to feel like I was part of the family. I never did. . . .
I needed to spend more time with my caseworker — one, not ten. I had a
new one every year. I needed to feel like someone cared about me. One
finally became concerned. I could tell she really cared. It was so neat. . . .
I stayed with one family for a month — that month was the neatest of
my whole life. I felt I belonged. This family trusted their kids and us. I
would have loved to stay with them, but it never occurred to me to ask if I
could. . . .
I'm still looking for a family to belong to. I've never had anyone I could
call Mom and Dad. I've always felt like a misfit. . . .
I don't think your study will make any difference. Things will go on as
they always have. I don't have much hope it will change, and you know why?
If you could change it, something would probably happen because you're
sitting here on this grass and talking with me. You know more what it's been
like for me in foster care. You can feel my emotions, my bitterness. But you
can't put me on paper to capture my emotions — what this has done to me.
If the big guys in Washington who could make a difference would talk to us,
things might change. But by the time this report gets to them, it'll only be so
many words on paper.[6]

Communications like this would tend to strengthen the will of
federal policymakers working to change the foster care system,
even though foster care was — and is — primarily a state responsibility. Although they were responsible for foster care, the states
had left the system in a tragic mess. Two years after this SDA
report, in the Adoption Assistance and Child Welfare Act of 1980,
the "big guys in Washington" changed federal child welfare laws
to create new incentives for finding permanent homes for foster
children, either through adoptions or through long-term foster
care placements. If the block grant enthusiasts don't succeed in
killing the new foster care and adoption opportunities program,
the lives of many foster children may be better.

## Presentation of Findings and Recommendations

SDA findings are presented through very brief reports (the goal
is twelve to fifteen pages, plus a few pages of appendices) and
through a series of briefings to program and agency managers, to
key Department and agency staff, and to the Secretary or Under
Secretary and top Department managers. The Secretary and the
others typically read the SDA report before the briefing. The
briefings typically take twenty minutes, leaving approximately
forty minutes for discussion.

The written reports include highlights of major findings, the purpose of the SDA, the issues examined, the methods used to gather data, and the SDA design; they may include descriptions of best practices observed. (Because of Freedom of Information Act requirements, recommendations are not included in the SDA reports but are instead presented as a separate list.) SDA findings include "descriptions (program origins and history, activities, reality of the local level), comparisons (trends, differences), and interpretations (relationships, possible causes and consequences)."[7] The SDA reports often illustrate the findings with anecdotes, direct quotes, examples of activities and events, or photographs of real situations.

Draft reports are circulated within the Department before the report is presented to the Secretary.

SDA briefings present the Secretary and top Department managers with firsthand feedback from the field, including the status of service delivery, conditions under which the program is operating, problems, and recommended changes in policy or program operations. Introduced by the Inspector General, who is responsible for leadership and quality control of the SDA program, an SDA staff member from the lead region presents the service delivery assessment findings and recommendations. The briefing serves as the occasion for substantive discussions among the Secretary, the SDA staff, program managers, and others present.[8]

## MANAGEMENT USES OF SERVICE DELIVERY ASSESSMENT

Service delivery assessments are used to inform the Secretary, Under Secretary, and other top Department managers about operating-level program reality. In this, SDAs have clearly been successful. Already, three Secretaries of Health and Human Services (HHS) have found SDAs sufficiently useful to put time aside to choose SDA topics, to be briefed on SDA findings, and to use SDA results.

Though researchers, evaluators, and policy analysts have tended to worry over the possible invalidity or unreliability of SDA findings, top managers in the Department have found the SDA information useful both in providing better understanding of programs funded or operated by the Department and in identifying operational problems and opportunities for management improvements.

One of Secretary Califano's priorities, for example, was to improve the management of the Department's programs. The first SDA, an assessment of the Head Start program, uncovered a serious management problem: failure to set priorities. The SDA report developed the issues as follows:

> Federal expressions of policy through performance standards, self-assessment and comprehensive management reviews receive endorsement and appreciation from program directors, staff and teachers. Their backing is tempered, however, with sincere concern over the mounting administrative burdens. . . .
>
> Local programs understand that the annual Self-Assessment Validation Instrument (SAVI) provides management at all levels with a means of assuring accountability and conformity with program objectives. However, program staff (69 percent of the programs) and parents who have participated in the SAVI agreed that the instrument is too complex, unnecessarily rigid and too lengthy. . . .
>
> Issue #6   Self-Assessment Validation Instrument (SAVI)
>
> There is a widespread program sentiment that while SAVI is a valuable management tool, the administrative burden is excessive. Programs complain of the "all or nothing" definition of compliance, and the lack of fiscal incentives to make improvements. Small programs are especially overwhelmed by the 162 compliance items. Some suggestions raised by program staff for improvements are to: (a) establish priority items for compliance, simplify instructions, and clarify the language used, (b) develop guidelines for compliance, allowing for degrees of compliance, and making provisions for program enrollment size, and (c) target funding increases or expansion monies to those programs with exceptional compliance records or those having severe compliance problems due to low funding levels.[9]

Head Start aims to provide comprehensive educational, health, nutrition, social services, parent involvement, and other services. Even for a multicomponent program like Head Start, Secretary Califano thought that 162 objectives were excessive. As one of his management initiatives, Secretary Califano stimulated the implementation of a much smaller set of program performance indicators that could be used to assess Head Start performance and results at grantee, regional, and national levels:

I'd like you to put together 25 key indicators by which you'd measure Head Start programs. . . . What are the 25 indicators of a good Head Start program. . . ? I want within 30 days 25 measures, because I'm going to start measuring. . . . By December, I'll have measured a substantial segment of Head Start programs.[10]

Development and implementation of the Head Start performance indicators took several months and substantial in-house and contract resources — but gave federal officials management tools that could be used both to document Head Start accomplishments and to stimulate better performance and results at national, regional, and grantee levels.

Though the service delivery assessment function has been curtailed with cutbacks in the size of the HHS workforce, the function continues to provide useful information to top department managers.

## EXAMPLE: MEDICARE CLIENTS' RELATIONSHIPS WITH FISCAL INTERMEDIARIES

The following example of useful evaluation work, which I watched unfold from my vantage point as an adviser to the HEW service delivery assessment program, should explain my enthusiasm for service delivery assessment.

Early in 1979 the Social Security Administration (SSA) and the new Health Care Financing Administration (HCFA), two of HEW's principal operating components, had agreed that (because of high workload in SSA district offices and increasing capability in HCFA) SSA district office staff would phase out of their role in assisting Medicare beneficiaries in getting reimbursements for their medical expenses. The HCFA intended that HCFA's fiscal intermediaries (Blue Cross and other carriers) would provide the necessary assistance to Medicare clients, primarily through toll-free telephone assistance. A service delivery assessment, "Medicare Clients' Relationships with Fiscal Intermediaries," provided early warning of impending problems in the proposed change, though.

The service delivery assessment focused on Medicare Part B (coverage for physicians' services), since it is in Part B that Medicare beneficiaries come into direct contact with carriers. Led by the Office of Service Delivery Assessment from HEW's Chicago region, the SDA team interviewed 325 elderly people at fifteen senior centers and nutrition sites in Illinois, Indiana, and California; they also interviewed thirty staff members who helped beneficiaries with Medicare-related problems at those sites. In addition, the SDA team did a review of the relevant literature; visited eight SSA district offices, one SSA teleservice center, and three carriers (in Milwaukee, Indianapolis, and Los Angeles); interviewed HCFA and SSA staff in the Boston, Philadelphia, and San Francisco regions; and reviewed 160 case files in the Chicago and San Francisco HCFA regional offices.[11]

The service delivery assessment, a fourteen-page report with ten pages of attachments, showed that (1) Medicare beneficiaries need face-to-face help in filing Medicare reimbursement claims; (2) most Medicare beneficiaries know of, and like, the personal help provided by Social Security district offices in the Medicare reimbursement process; (3) most Medicare beneficiaries do not know who their carrier is or what its role is in Medicare.

Key findings were presented under five headings: Profile of Beneficiaries, Beneficiary Attitudes about Medicare, Beneficiary Experiences with Carriers, Carrier Experiences with Beneficiaries, and Relationships between HCFA and SSA.

### Profile of Beneficiaries

The Medicare beneficiaries that we spoke with were all elderly — over 65 years old, mostly hard of hearing and poor in eyesight, many with debilitating health problems and some who had recently lost a spouse. We think particularly of the 80-year-old woman in the Senior Citizens Center who talked nonstop in a rather confused, nervous manner about her dying husband. She had a handful of medical bills with no understanding of what to do with them or even what questions she could ask. We can also vividly recall the elderly gentleman in the Social Security district office who brought in medical bills for himself and his wife, unable to decipher which expenses were covered by Medicare, which by his supplemental policy and which he would have to pay for himself. And then there was the very angry man who understood how to submit his Medicare claims, but who was deeply frustrated by not getting paid the 80% he expected; and, to him, the two Explanation of Medicare Benefits (EOMB) forms that he held in his hand were incomprehensible.

Mostly, we recall confused, disappointed, frightened and angry people who couldn't get a handle on the Medicare system at a time in their lives when their physical and financial resources were dwindling.[12]

### Beneficiary Attitudes about Medicare

Responses from beneficiaries were remarkably consistent. The vast majority did not or could not talk about their carrier but rather about the Medicare program in general. Most completely fail to understand the role of the carrier in Medicare and have no relationship at all with a carrier other than in claims processing. At a Senior Center site in East Los Angeles, there wasn't a single beneficiary who even knew the name Occidental.[13]

Many associate a local SSA district office with "the Medicare," going there for information and assistance.[14]

### Beneficiary Experiences with Carriers

As noted previously, few of the beneficiaries understood what a carrier was or how it functioned.[15]

The vast majority of beneficiaries spoke of a need to get help in submitting their bills. Typical complaints were: (1) "I'm not used to filling out government forms, I'm afraid I won't do it right"; (2) "I don't know what to do with the bottom half of the form"; (3) "The doctor doesn't put the right information on his bill." While the 1490 does not seem to be frightening for those accustomed to filling out government forms, many beneficiaries are, in fact, intimidated by it. One carrier noted that 70% of its walk-in business dealt with the submission of the 1490. SSA district office staff consistently said that over half their Medicare walk-in traffic related to the submission of claims.[16]

One carrier official noted that the beneficiaries were at a real disadvantage in dealing with the carrier through correspondence since beneficiaries frequently were unsure of their questions and not familiar with the proper jargon.[17]

### Carrier Experiences with Beneficiaries

Carrier staff confirmed much of what beneficiaries said. They said that: (1) physical accessibility is the key to effectively serving a significant percentage of beneficiaries; (2) beneficiaries find it necessary to bring in claims forms to make sure that they're doing things right and that forms get to the right place; (3) correspondence is not an effective way to deal with beneficiaries, since issues can be very complicated and beneficiaries may have difficulty expressing themselves clearly; (4) the telephone is more effective than correspondence, although Medicare-related calls take much more time than private-insurance-related calls since the program is very complex and many beneficiaries "just want to have someone to talk to."[18]

### Relationships between HCFA and SSA

Despite the understanding of staff at both agencies that SSA is phasing out of its information and assistance role to Medicare beneficiaries (other than in entitlement), the fact remains that many beneficiaries not only continue to visit district offices for help but equate Social Security offices with "the federal government" and, to a lesser extent, with Medicare.

Since beneficiaries enroll in Medicare at district offices and pay their premiums through the Social Security system, it seems problematic that beneficiaries will easily be persuaded to contact a carrier rather than the district office after entitlement. Furthermore, there do not appear to be plans to enable carriers to set up local offices to serve beneficiaries. Hence the type of personal contact which most beneficiaries feel they need will not be provided by carriers. While the volume of Medicare business differs among the SSA district offices (e.g., district offices located in high Medicaid areas do not have a very high Medicare workload) and while many staff would welcome being relieved of the Medicare workload, almost all service reps recognized that Medicare beneficiaries would continue to come to the district office for help.

It seems highly likely that, despite sophisticated toll-free telephone systems or correspondence mechanisms, beneficiaries will continue to come to SSA district offices for assistance. One carrier employee commented that it seemed strange to him that HEW would take the most complicated program (Medicare) out of the SSA district offices and make the beneficiaries of that program rely upon the telephone as its primary communication link with the system.[19]

Early in 1979 policymakers far from the public were about to reduce Medicare services dramatically. As a result of this service delivery assessment, however, the Department of Health, Education, and Welfare reversed the tentative decision to phase out face-to-face Social Security district office assistance to Medicare beneficiaries. The plan to rely primarily on toll-free telephone assistance, which had been approved at SSA and HCFA levels, was reversed at Department level.

## ORGANIZATION AND MANAGEMENT OF THE SDA PROGRAM

In the Department of Health and Human Services, the Inspector General serves as functional manager of the SDA program, managing development of the SDA work plan, maintaining quality control, and bringing SDA findings to the attention of the Secretary and other top managers in the Department. Service delivery assessments are conducted by federal staff from the ten HHS regional offices.[20]

The Secretary selects and assigns the SDA studies, typically selecting several topics from a proposed annual work plan recommended by the Inspector General on the basis of recommendations from throughout the Department, and adding other topics not on the recommended list. Other SDAs are conducted when the Secretary requests quick assessments on high-priority topics.

A number of other agencies have plans to test the service delivery assessment approach. In the Department of Education, service delivery assessments have been assigned to the Division of Performance Management Systems, which also conducts evaluability assessments, rapid-feedback evaluations, and program management reviews.

## CONCLUSION

Though service delivery assessment uses the combination of qualitative and quantitative methods characteristic of evaluability assessment and rapid-feedback evaluation, service delivery assessment tends to be much less goal-oriented than either of those evaluation approaches. Service delivery assessment provides much richer data on program reality than is obtained in the typical goal-oriented evaluation, though service delivery assessment suffers from lack of direction as to which questions are of greatest interest.

One of my dreams has been to combine the goal-oriented evaluability assessment and the goal-free service delivery assessment processes, quickly producing what I believe would be extremely powerful management-oriented evaluations. The Department of Education has accomplished this by doing some of their service delivery assessments as followups to evaluability assessments. At an early opportunity, I plan to test this combination myself.

We now turn to an outcome-oriented extension of management by objectives (MBO), examining a simple evaluation process that is a necessary component of any results-oriented management system.

## NOTES TO CHAPTER 6

1. Michael Hendricks and James Bell provided very helpful comments on earlier drafts of this chapter.

2. Michael Hendricks, Office of the Inspector General, U.S. Department of Health and Human Services, July 29, 1981 (personal communication).

3. See *Service Delivery Assessment Training Manual* (U.S. Department of Health and Human Services, Office of the Inspector General, July 1981, draft); Michael Hendricks, "Service Delivery Assessment: Qualitative Evaluation at the Cabinet Level," in N. L. Smith, ed., *Federal Efforts to Develop New Evaluation Methods, New Directions for Program Evaluation,* no. 12 (San Francisco: Jossey-Bass, December 1981), pp. 5–24; and Michael Hendricks, "Oral Policy Briefings," in N. L. Smith, ed., *Alternative Forms of Representation in Evaluation* (Beverly Hills, Calif.: Sage Publications, forthcoming).

4. *Service Delivery Assessment Training Manual,* p. 7-14.

5. *Service Delivery Assessment Training Manual,* p. 5-9.

6. *Foster Care Assessment: Executive Report* (U.S. Department of Health, Education, and Welfare, Office of Service Delivery Assessment, Regions VII and X, with II, V, VI, October 1978), p. i.

7. *Service Delivery Assessment Training Manual,* p. 9-2.

8. See Michael Hendricks, "Oral Policy Briefings."

9. *Head Start Assessment* (U.S. Department of Health, Education, and Welfare, Office of Service Delivery Assessment, Region III, with I, IV, VII, IX, and X, May 1978, pp. 11-12.

10. Joseph A. Califano, Jr., Secretary of Health, Education, and Welfare, responding to the Head Start SDA briefing, May 19, 1978.

11. *Service Delivery Assessment of Medicare Clients' Relationships with Fiscal Intermediaries* (Chicago: U.S. Department of Health, Education, and Welfare, Office of Service Delivery Assessment, Region V, March 1979), p. 4.

12. Ibid., p. 5.

13. Ibid., p. 5.

14. Ibid., p. 6.

15. Ibid., p. 7.

16. Ibid., p. 8.

17. Ibid., p. 11.

18. Ibid., p. 11.

19. Ibid., pp. 13–14.

20. This section is based on the *Service Delivery Assessment Training Manual,* Chapter 1, and discussions with Michael Hendricks.

# 7

## Outcome
## Monitoring

## INTRODUCTION

Government managers manage public programs as they manage their own lives, attempting to improve performance by adjusting activities when performance leaves too much to be desired. To achieve improved program results by this method, managers need some way to get systematic feedback on program outcomes. To achieve demonstrably effective programs, moreover, managers need ways both to get systematic feedback on program outcomes and to communicate program outcomes to others.

Central to results-oriented management is the very simple form of evaluation known variously as outcome monitoring, performance measurement, performance monitoring, or impact monitoring. Building on a framework of agreed-on, outcome-oriented program objectives and quantitative or qualitative performance measures (a definition of program performance developed through evaluability assessment and rapid-feedback evaluation or by other means), *outcome monitoring* measures program performance in terms of the agreed-on objectives and performance measures; it then compares program performance with prior performance or with standards of expected performance. (Since our main emphasis is on the monitoring of program outcomes, we use the term *outcome monitoring* here. In other writings we have used the term *performance monitoring*. Whatever term is used, both process measures and outcome measures will be important in the types of monitoring systems with which we are concerned in this chapter.)

Establishment of an appropriate outcome monitoring system moves programs to Level 2 on the results-oriented management scale introduced in Chapter 1 (Table 1-1) and lays the basis for policy and management agreement on realistic performance targets (Level 3 performance).

Evaluation has gotten a bad name because evaluation too often fails to produce timely, relevant information on program performance. Evaluation research typically begins with great hopes, saying or implying that:

> Through collection and analysis of suitable data, the evaluation will determine to what extent program activities are effective, and will show what works best under what conditions.[1]

Months or years later, often well beyond the originally promised completion date, evaluation researchers too often produce inconclusive reports, together with complaints and excuses regarding the unavailability of needed data on program activities and results, unavailability of needed comparison data, and lack of communication with decision makers.

Together with qualitative case studies (see Chapters 5 and 6), outcome monitoring is usually the most feasible evaluation alternative. Less ambitious than evaluation research, outcome monitoring simply measures program outcomes and progress toward program objectives, leaving to others the task of estimating the extent to which program activities have caused the observed results. This chapter, after briefly describing the outcome monitoring process, explores the prospects for establishing outcome monitoring systems for typical government programs.

## THE OUTCOME MONITORING PROCESS

The prerequisite for a useful outcome monitoring system is management's agreement on an appropriate set of program objectives (including important side effects to be minimized) and the availability of a set of qualitative or quantitative outcome measures in terms of which the program is to be assessed and managed.

Chapters 2 and 3 presented one method for getting policy and management agreement on an appropriate set of program objectives. In Chapter 5, we suggested how appropriate outcome measures can be developed. As was indicated in those chapters, appropriate objectives and performance measures must be both relevant to policy and management interests and grounded in the reality of program operations.

Given management's agreement on an appropriate set of program objectives and outcome measures, outcome monitoring is a four-step process: (1) establishment of data sources; (2) collection of data on program outcomes; (3) comparison of program outcomes with prior or expected outcomes; and (4) assisting policy and management decisions. Each step is described in the next sections.

## Establishment of Data Sources

Typical sources of program performance data include agency and program records, existing data systems, use of trained observers, and conduct of special surveys. Since agency and program records often lack program outcome data, special surveys or site visits will often be required to get such data (see Chapter 5).

In project-grant programs, access to necessary data can usually be arranged most easily when a proposed project is under review. In ongoing programs, access to new data often requires prolonged negotiations, which may be facilitated by evaluability assessments or other efforts to build consensus on appropriate sets of objectives and performance indicators.

Chapter 9 suggests incentives that might be used to motivate provision of, or access to, needed program outcome data.

## Collection of Data on Program Outcomes

Given agreement on program outcome measures and access to needed data, the data collection should be relatively straightforward. The term *outcome monitoring* connotes repetitive, ongoing data collection; for example, on a quarterly basis. In contrast to one-shot evaluation studies, outcome monitoring provides opportunities to revise and perfect data collection systems; and it motivates those in the field by feeding back data comparing the performance of different organizational units.

As suggested in Chapter 5, using a combination of data collection methods ensures that valid program performance data are obtained. Representative samples will often be used to obtain reliable estimates of program accomplishments at reasonable cost. A formal system will often be required to check on the validity and reliability of the program performance data.

## Comparison of Program Outcomes with Prior or Expected Outcomes

Outcome monitoring provides one or more of the following comparisons: (1) comparison of program performance with prior performance; (2) comparison of program performance with some standard of expected performance; (3) intra-program comparisons.

### Comparison of Program Performance with Prior Performance

As an ongoing management tool, outcome monitoring focuses the attention of all management levels on key dimensions of program performance; in particular, on important program outcomes. The key comparisons will often be the outcomes in the preceding quarter or preceding year: "Last year, we scored 63 [on some relevant scale]; this year we achieved a 79."

### Comparison of Program Performance with Some Standard of Expected Performance

When realistic target levels of expected program outcome have been developed (using data on past program performance or data on comparable programs), outcome monitoring compares actual program outcomes with those standards: "Our performance target was 75; we achieved a 79."

### Intra-Program Comparisons

Outcome monitoring typically gathers sufficient data to make possible comparisons of the performance of different organizational units within the program: "Among projects in the rural

South, projects A, B, and C achieved scores of 42, 85, and 61, respectively." Such comparisons can trigger qualitative case studies to document how the high performers achieved especially good results — and to trigger management actions to stimulate improvements in program and project results.

## Assisting Policy and Management Decisions

As in other management-oriented evaluation, the objective of outcome monitoring is to assist policy and management decisions on program resources, program activities, program objectives, and collection and use of program performance information. Since outcome monitoring reports have the same form as typical management reports (though they provide outcome data not usually found in management reports), outcome monitoring provides a familiar vehicle for policy and management decisions.

## EXAMPLES OF OUTCOME MONITORING SYSTEMS

Chapter 1 discussed systems used to monitor results achieved by the Bureau of Community Health Services, the Head Start program, the Guaranteed Student Loan program, and the Harlem Valley Psychiatric Center. Chapter 5 examined a flexible system used by the Bureau of Health Planning to monitor progress toward varying sets of objectives in a multiobjective program. *Performance Measurement, Developing Client Outcome Monitoring Systems,* and *Evaluation: Promise and Performance* present many other examples of outcome monitoring systems used by local, state, and federal agencies.[2]

Here we review a system that was used to monitor the performance and results of high-priority Department of Health, Education, and Welfare (HEW) programs; we then examine prospects for developing appropriate monitoring systems in a "soft" program area, mental health.

## Major Initiatives Tracking System (MITS)

Since the time of Elliot Richardson, Secretary of Health, Education, and Welfare in the Nixon administration, every HEW Secretary has had a system for tracking progress on initiatives of particular interest to the Secretary. From the points of view of those served by HEW programs, most of those tracking systems have been process-oriented (monitoring development and enactment of legislative proposals, for example).

Early in his tour as Secretary, Joseph A. Califano, Jr., established a performance monitoring system, the Major Initiatives Tracking System (MITS), which was designed to focus HEW management and staff efforts on priority improvements in the services provided by HEW programs. Secretary Califano's system focused, to the extent possible, on end results to be achieved.[3]

Though the Major Initiatives Tracking System was by no means perfect, it did focus the attention of top Department managers on achieving demonstrable improvements in program performance and results. By 1979 MITS was tracking the performance and results of 50 HEW programs, comparing actual program performance with quarterly targets of expected performance on a total of 160 performance measures. By the end of his tour in the Department, Secretary Califano was able to report performance improvements in many HEW programs, as follows:

In health:

— We led a national campaign to immunize all American children (5–14 years of age) against the six preventable childhood diseases. We set and the Department will meet the goal of immunizing 90% of all children by October 1, 1979. We have already reduced reported cases of measles by 78%, rubella by 43%, and mumps by 30% through June 1979 as compared to 1977. . . .[4]

In education:

— We proposed and Congress enacted a massive expansion of student assistance grant and loan programs to provide more help to students from lower- and middle-income families. . . .
— We brought OE's six programs of student financial assistance together in one bureau, and managed them aggressively for the first time.
— In the $2.1 billion Basic Grant Program, we saved $222 million by initiating a computer-based review and validation of applications that screened out nearly 500,000 ineligible students.
— In the $1.0 billion Guaranteed Student Loan Program, we have put over 80,000 loans into repayment status, with a total dollar value of $115 million, and reduced the backlog of unworked default accounts from 400,000 to 237,000.[5]

## In the Social Security Administration:

— Working in harmony with state governments, we reduced the error rate in the AFDC program from 8.6% as of July 30, 1977 to 7.1% as of September 30, 1978 saving $90 million in Federal outlays in the current fiscal year.

— We made equally dramatic gains in the federally managed SSI program reducing the error rate from 6.3% as of March 30, 1977 to 4.6% as of September 30, 1978, also a savings of $90 million in the current year.

These two management improvements have yielded overall savings of $340,000,000 since 1977.

— In the SSI program, we reduced the average time required to process a claim for an aged recipient by 47% — from 34 days to 18 days as of March 31, 1979;

— In the Disability Insurance Program, we increased the overall accuracy on initial claims processing from 83.5% to 92.1% as of March 31, 1979;

— In the Child Support Enforcement Program, since January 1977 we have collected and distributed more than $1 billion in child support payments for welfare mothers and children, and have increased collections at the annual rate of 48% during the 12 months ending December 31, 1979.[6]

## In civil rights:

— We doubled the workforce and tripled the number of cases closed by each investigator in the Office for Civil Rights and will eliminate by September 30, 1979, the backlog of about 2,000 complaints of sex and race discrimination that we inherited.[7]

Even where managers lack authority to achieve performance targets through their own resources (a typical situation in public programs), an outcome monitoring system can focus management attention on the directions in which policymakers wish to move the program. In the week before he left office, Secretary Califano was still working on this problem. He suggested a process that would be appropriate in many government programs:

HEW managers are responsible for program leadership, whether they have sole control over their programs or whether they share the administrative responsibilities with State and local officials. . . .

Specific Actions

1. Department officials with responsibilities for programs administered by State or local governments will phase in, working with these units of government, measurable objectives and expected results. These objectives should set performance targets that each level of government will

strive to attain over a reasonable period of time, say one to two years. . . .

2. The Assistant Secretary for Management and Budget will modify the MITS procedures to ensure that current and future initiatives monitored under MITS, which involve State and/or local administration, include actions Federal officials will undertake to implement this policy. . . .

4. The Assistant Secretary for Personnel will ensure that personal performance evaluations include, where appropriate, an assessment of a Federal manager's: (a) success in reaching agreement with State program officials on program objectives; (b) achievement of the objectives; and (c) approach to assist these officials in meeting the objectives. . . .[8]

## Mental Health Programs

Mental health programs are "soft": relatively difficult to measure. If outcome monitoring systems can be developed for mental health programs, therefore, it should be possible to develop appropriate outcome monitoring systems for most government programs.[9]

In Chapter 1, we examined an outcome monitoring system for a single mental institution under a single manager, the Harlem Valley Psychiatric Center. Here we turn our attention to the feasibility of developing appropriate outcome monitoring systems for less centralized mental health programs.

Community mental health centers, funded from multiple sources, face competing sets of priorities (Chapter 1, Table 1-2) and consequent difficulty in demonstrating effective performance. Still, it appears that there are enough similarities in the dimensions of interest to different funding sources to allow development of a common core of performance measures appropriate at all levels of government.

The Mental Health Systems Act of 1980 required that the Secretary of Health and Human Services "prescribe standard measures of performance to test the quality and extent of performance by the recipients of grants and contracts . . . and the extent to which such performance has helped to achieve the national or other objectives for which the grants or contracts were made or entered into."[10] In response to this law and other pressures toward greater accountability, the National Institute of Mental Health (NIMH) developed a number of performance indicators for the community mental health center (CMHC) program, including the following:

proportion of the population with access to CMHC services; admission rates for minorities, children, and elderly people; severely mentally disabled patients as a proportion of total caseload; indicators of financial viability (for example, amount collected as a proportion of amount billed); and indicators of efficiency/productivity.[11] These performance measures appear appropriate to state and local mental health programs as well. As is so often the case, however, federal managers did not achieve agreement on measures of quality of care or of service outcome (though NIMH had tested client-impact indicators in Oregon and other states through state- and federally-funded demonstration projects[12]).

In an exciting piece of work, Alfred Schainblatt and Harry Hatry have developed performance measures that could be used to provide outcome data on clients served by community mental health programs. Their outcome monitoring system used mail questionnaires with follow-up telephone calls to get three- or six-month follow-up data on client distress, social functioning (at home, on the job, and in the community), and client satisfaction. In contrast with the high-cost personal interviewing used in other client outcome monitoring systems being tested at state level, Schainblatt and Hatry's system was less expensive and attained higher response rates. In tests with the Arlington County (Virginia) Division of Mental Health Services and the Michigan Department of Mental Health, response rates ranged from 68% to 82%.[13]

Using the performance indicators mentioned above, managers and their staffs could develop systems for monitoring the performance and results of mental health programs at federal, state, or local level. Both process measures and outcome measures could be used. The performance measures could be used to set performance targets for state or local mental health programs (for example, target levels for the proportion of clients whose ability to function on the job is significantly increased following treatment). Performance measures and performance standards would vary from state to state and from locality to locality. (Even before the federal community mental health centers program was transformed into a block grant program in the 1981 budget reconciliation act, imposition of uniform national performance standards would not, in my judgment, have been appropriate.)

## MANAGEMENT USES OF OUTCOME MONITORING

Outcome monitoring systems communicate results-to-be-achieved throughout a program or organization. As we will see in Chapter 9, use of outcome-oriented performance targets appears to motivate improved performance ("I'm building a cathedral!").

If managers wish to manage for results, some form of outcome monitoring system will be required. Periodic monitoring reports will allow managers to compare program performance with prior or expected performance; to identify intra-program variations in performance (for example, performance variations among regions, among states, among localities, or among centers directly serving clients); to identify problem areas; to identify high performers whose exploits might be worthy of documentation; and to suggest management actions that will improve program or project performance and results.

Outcome monitoring also lays the basis for subsequent "interrupted time series" evaluations of program effectiveness (see Chapter 5) by providing program outcome data on a monthly, quarterly, or annual basis.

## CONCLUSION

This chapter completes our examination of methods for defining expected program performance and obtaining relatively inexpensive assessments of program performance. We now turn our attention to other activities needed for the implementation of effective evaluation and management systems.

## NOTES TO CHAPTER 7

1. Most of us have heard — or sung — this song before.

2. See *Performance Measurement: A Guide for Local Elected Officials* (Washington, D.C.: The Urban Institute Press, 1980); Rhona Millar and others, *Developing Client Outcome Monitoring Systems: A Guide for State and Local Social Services Agencies* (Washington, D.C.: The Urban Institute, 1981); and Joseph S. Wholey, *Evaluation: Promise and Performance* (Washington, D.C.: The Urban Institute, 1979).

3. Memorandum from Joseph A. Califano, Jr., Secretary of Health, Education, and Welfare, "Major Initiatives Tracking System," July 28, 1979).

4. Memorandum from Joseph A. Califano, Jr., Secretary of Health, Education, and Welfare, July 26, 1979, p. 3.

5. Ibid., p. 5.

6. Ibid., pp. 6-7.

7. Ibid., p. 7.

8. Memorandum from Joseph A. Califano, Jr., Secretary of Health, Education, and Welfare, "The Accountability of Federal Managers for Results in State-Administered Programs," July 27, 1979.

9. This section returns to a line of inquiry developed in my paper "Results Oriented Management: Integrating Evaluation and Organizational Performance Incentives," in Gerald J. Stahler and William R. Tash, eds., *Innovative Approaches to Mental Health Evaluation* (New York: Academic Press, 1982), pp. 255-275. I am grateful to those who commented on that paper, especially Michael Jewell, Murray Levine, Alfred Schainblatt, Steven Scharfstein, and J. Richard Woy.

10. *The Mental Health Systems Act of 1980, P.L. 96-398* (October 7, 1980), Section 316, "Performance Standards."

11. See "The Revised Management System for Federally Funded Community Mental Health Centers," National Insitutue of Mental Health working paper, n.d. (1980).

12. Michael Jewell, Office of the Assistant Secretary for Planning and Evaluation, U.S. Department of Health and Human Services, personal communication, November 1980. See "The Oregon Health System — A Framework for Systematic Program Analysis" and other reports available from the National Institute of Mental Health.

13. See Alfred H. Schainblatt and Harry P. Hatry, *Mental Health Services: What Happens to the Clients?* (Washington, D.C.: The Urban Institute, 1979), and Alfred H. Schainblatt, "What Happens to the Clients? Monitoring Outcomes of State and Local Mental Health Services," Paper presented at the Annual Meeting of the Evaluation Research Society, Minneapolis, Minn., October 1979.

PART

Using Evaluation
to Stimulate
Effective Management

# 8

# Implementing a Management-Oriented Evaluation Program

## INTRODUCTION

In Chapter 1 we suggested that evaluators and other analysts should place priority on management-oriented evaluation activities designed to help produce agreement on sets of results-oriented program objectives and performance indicators, to produce evidence on program performance in terms of the agreed-on objectives and performance indicators, and to help produce demonstrable improvements in the design and performance of government agencies and programs. Succeeding chapters examined specific management-oriented evaluation approaches.

In this chapter we will review the five types of activities needed to implement a management-oriented evaluation program: establishing and communicating a clear evaluation policy; mobilizing needed resources; demonstrating desired evaluation activities; persuading and assisting; and monitoring evaluation activities and results. We briefly discuss a sixth set of activities designed to enhance the effectiveness of management-oriented evaluation programs: linking evaluation to other management support functions.[1]

The discussion draws on experiences in the U.S. Department of Health, Education, and Welfare (HEW), which is now the Department of Health and Human Services (HHS), between 1978 and 1980. At that time, approximately forty HEW/HHS units were carrying out evaluations, at an annual cost of more than $40 million.[2]

## SETTING EVALUATION POLICY

In many agencies, *evaluation* is an undefined term. The first step in establishing an effective evaluation program is to develop a clear policy on how evaluation resources are to be used, what types of evaluation activities are to be given priority, and what results are expected from evaluation. Since both managers and evaluators tend to be unhappy with past evaluation efforts, finding them time-consuming but seldom very useful, it will often be easy to get agreement that changes in evaluation activities are in order. In 1978, for example, the Department of Health, Education, and Welfare set new directions that placed increasing emphasis on short-term management-oriented evaluations designed to improve the design and performance of HEW programs. The new directions put particular emphasis on evaluation activities that would assist managers and policymakers in setting realistic measurable objectives for their programs. The Under Secretary's guidance for fiscal year 1979 HEW evaluation activities contained this statement:

> During FY 1979, I want the timeliness and usefulness of evaluation projects improved. The Secretary and I have been impressed with the value of the quick turn-around service delivery assessments conducted by Regional Offices under the general direction of the Inspector General. I have asked the Assistant Secretary for Planning and Evaluation to work with you to shorten the time duration of evaluation projects and to improve the utilization of evaluation findings. In my view, the most important initial step is the identification of realistic measurable objectives and outcome-oriented performance measures on which the program will be held accountable. . . .
>
> During the coming year, the Assistant Secretary for Planning and Evaluation will be working with you to begin to identify the realistic measurable objectives and important side-effects (indicators of program performance) on which the Department's programs will be held accountable. The Assistant Secretary for Planning and Evaluation will also be developing evaluation standards and providing training and technical assistance to agency managers and their staffs.[3]

In subsequent years the Department's evaluation planning system was modified to accelerate the desired types of evaluation activities, and subordinate agencies were directed to reallocate resources from research-oriented to management-oriented evaluations. The Under Secretary's guidance for fiscal year 1980 and fiscal year 1981 evaluation activities put increasing emphasis on the desired changes in evaluation focus:

Managers and evaluators are to give high priority to activities designed to clarify program goals, identify appropriate program performance indicators, and document what is known about program performance in terms of those indicators. To facilitate these activities, approval of certain evaluations is delegated to agency heads.[4]

Principal Operating Components[5] are to give high priority to program performance evaluations designed to clarify program objectives and to assess program performance in terms of those objectives. In FY 1980, the Department made important progress in the initiation of these efforts. For FY 1981, each Principal Operating Component should develop a two-to-four-year schedule for completion of program performance evaluations for all its programs. At least 30% of POC/agency evaluation resources are to be devoted to such evaluations. To facilitate these activities, approval of evaluability assessments costing less than $100,000 is again delegated to agency heads.[6]

## MOBILIZING THE NECESSARY RESOURCES

In HEW, a key initial step was the creation of a new Office of Evaluation and Technical Analysis (hereafter referred to as the "Office of Evaluation") headed by a deputy assistant secretary in the Office of the Assistant Secretary for Planning and Evaluation (ASPE). Even before the new Office of Evaluation was formally established, actions were taken to mobilize necessary resources. These actions included assembling the best staff that could be quickly put together, hiring six contractors who would carry out management-oriented evaluations under task orders to be developed for specific evaluations, and beginning the training of staff and contractors in management-oriented evaluation.

With staff positions limited, the necessary evaluation staff were assembled through transfers within ASPE and within the Department, through details of two staff members from universities and two from state governments under the Intergovernmental Personnel Act, through use of temporary and term positions, and through use of contractors. Contractors were selected under two-year contracts, each of which provided for a series of short-term evaluations (evaluability assessments and rapid-feedback evaluations) under task orders to be developed for each evaluation. To facilitate timely initiation of evaluability assessments, the Office of Evaluation developed a generalized task order specifying activities to be undertaken and products to be produced. Information was included in each task order specifying the program to be evaluated and the time and resources available. To ensure the relevance of contract evaluation activities, each of these evaluations was guided by an Office of Evaluation staff member, a work group, and a policy group consisting of relevant program and policy staff.

When an evaluation approach is new to an organization, a good deal of training and technical assistance will be necessary to ensure that the approach is implemented effectively. In HEW, training and assistance were given to central Office of Evaluation staff, to agency staff, and to contractors through an ongoing evaluation seminar and a series of briefings and workshops for agency managers, evaluation staff, and contractors.

## DEMONSTRATING MANAGEMENT-ORIENTED EVALUATION

When introducing a new evaluation approach, it will be necessary for those in charge of evaluation activities to focus evaluation resources on a subset of agency programs. In HEW, ASPE decided to focus initial management-oriented evaluation activities on Public Health Service, Office of Education, and social services programs, where existing legislation provided that a small portion of program funds could be used by the Secretary for program evaluation. (At that time, and still today, the Office of the Secretary lacked resources for systematic evaluation of many of the programs funded under the Social Security Act.) Based on an agenda approved by the Under Secretary, the new Office of Evaluation undertook evaluations that provided assistance to managers of approximately twenty-five HEW programs.

In response to these efforts to demonstrate the value of management-oriented evaluation, the Public Health Service and the Department of Education have embarked on multiyear efforts to establish realistic measurable objectives for agency programs and to increase the emphasis placed on management-oriented evaluation activities.

## PERSUADING AND ASSISTING

In a large organization, policy-level guidance and directives are often dead letters. Informal efforts are needed to convince agency managers and evaluators that new evaluation directions make sense. Beginning in 1978, for example, staff in the HEW Office of Evaluation undertook an extensive missionary effort designed to sell the concepts of "management-oriented evaluation" and "demonstrably effective programs" throughout the Department. Included in this effort were three important sets of activities: presentations to line managers and executive staffs; periodic meetings with evaluation staffs throughout the Department; and the evaluation seminars and workshops mentioned earlier.

Important to the credibility of these missionary efforts were three changes in Department-level evaluation activities: acceleration and compression of the Department's lengthy process of evaluation planning and plan review; delegation to agency level (one or two levels below Department level) of approval of evaluability assessments costing less than $100,000; and provision of assistance to agency managers and policymakers.

The HEW Office of Evaluation provided assistance to Office of Human Development Services managers (for example, when OHDS was under pressure from the Secretary to develop performance indicators and a performance measurement system for the Head Start program). The Office of Evaluation provided assistance to U.S. Office of Education managers and policymakers in setting new directions for the Follow Through program and in responding to a congressional mandate to develop measurable objectives for all education programs.

## MONITORING EVALUATION ACTIVITIES AND RESULTS

In an evaluation program, evaluation activities can be monitored at the planning stage, while the evaluations are under way, and after evaluations are completed. In HEW, the Department's Office of Evaluation monitored and assisted agency evaluators at the planning stage, and it produced a number of reports documenting the extent to which evaluations had been used in policy development and program management. Most ongoing evaluations were monitored at agency or bureau level.

## Monitoring Evaluation Plans

As functional manager of the HEW/HHS evaluation program since 1967, the Assistant Secretary for Planning and Evaluation (ASPE) is expected to set standards for evaluation, to monitor evaluation activities throughout the Department, to review and approve agency evaluation plans and projects (most of which are undertaken under legislation authorizing use of up to 1 percent of certain program funds for program evaluation "by the Secretary"), and to encourage the semiautonomous agencies and bureaus to meet Departmental priorities.[7] As a result of its distance from most agency and bureau evaluation staffs and its having had relatively little evaluation staff of its own, ASPE's management of HEW evaluation was primarily a paper process prior to creation of the Office of Evaluation in 1978.

Since ASPE already had the power to review and approve agency evaluation plans and projects, it proved possible to bring the evaluation management function to life with the creation of a more adequately staffed Office of Evaluation within ASPE. At the evaluation planning stage, evaluation activities were monitored and given Departmental direction through a four-stage process: (1) early meetings between ASPE and agency evaluation staffs, to exchange and discuss "Evaluation Strategy Statement" (plans for evaluations to be undertaken in the coming year); (2) follow-up memoranda indicating which evaluation projects were likely to be approved; (3) a second round of meetings to review detailed descriptions of proposed evaluation projects; (4) ASPE memoranda indicating which evaluation projects were approved, which were disapproved, and which needed more discussion.[8]

The ASPE review of agency evaluation plans was intended to ensure the quality and relevance of proposed evaluations, and to avoid duplication or unnecessary overlapping of evaluation activities. By getting the evaluation planning process moving early, by undertaking joint (rather than sequential) agency evaluation plan reviews with the Public Health Service, the Office of Education, and the Office of Human Development Services, and by emphasizing the desirability of initiating evaluation projects early in the fiscal year, the Office of Evaluation was able to accelerate the evaluation planning process. More important, the human inter-action in the ongoing series of meetings allowed the Office of Evaluation to move agency and bureau evaluation offices in the desired direction — in this instance, toward management-oriented evaluation. (The availability of immediate help from Office of Evaluation staff and contractors was also important in getting agency evaluation offices moving toward management-oriented evaluation.)

## Monitoring Ongoing and Completed Evaluations

Sad as it may sound, evaluations often seem to disappear a short time after they have been completed. Since 1974 ASPE has solved this basic problem by operating an Evaluation Documentation Center, which collects, indexes, and disseminates information on completed and ongoing evaluations throughout the Department.[9] The Evaluation Documentation Center, besides publishing ab-stracts of completed and ongoing evaluations, operates a com-puterized indexing and retrieval system.

## Monitoring Utilization of Evaluation

With the following statement in July 1979, the Senate Appropria-tions Committee gave a helpful prod to ASPE efforts to monitor the usefulness of HEW evaluations:

> The Committee is unaware of any significant program improvements that have been brought about by the Department's large annual investment in evaluation contracts with consultant organizations. It seems as though, year after year, the same programs get re-evaluated, yet never change.[10]

In response to the Senate Appropriations Committee (which perceived the HEW evaluation program to be ineffective), the Office of Evaluation challenged evaluation staffs throughout the Department to produce counterexamples showing that the com-mittee was incorrect. By the time of the next appropriations cycle, key members of the Senate and House Appropriations Committees had been presented with a report on "Evaluation Utilization in the

Department of Health, Education, and Welfare."[11] This report presented twenty-one examples of HEW evaluations that had influenced legislative proposals, influenced program regulations, or helped bring about improvements in day-to-day program operations. In transmitting the evaluation utilization report to Congress, Patricia Roberts Harris, Secretary of Health and Human Services, noted that:

> Several of the studies cited have influenced legislative proposals, and many have contributed to improvement in program design and management.
>
> As Part II of the report indicates, it is now Departmental policy to devote more of its evaluation resources to program performance evaluations. The objectives of these evaluations are to produce evidence on the extent to which the Department's programs are achieving the results intended by the legislation and to inject greater accountability for such results into the management of HHS programs.[12]

The evaluation utilization report met its objective of convincing key appropriations committee staff that HHS evaluations were being used to redirect and improve HHS programs. The report also served as a vehicle for communicating the steps that had been taken to strengthen the Department's evaluation function and to bring together the Department's management, evaluation, and personnel administration systems.

As Chapter 4 showed, there have been a number of ad hoc assessments of the impact of the management-oriented evaluation approach, particularly in the U.S. Public Health Service. In fiscal year 1983, the Office of the Assistant Secretary for Planning and Evaluation acted to establish a system for ongoing monitoring of the results of completed evaluations.

## LINKING EVALUATION TO OTHER MANAGEMENT SUPPORT FUNCTIONS

Government is full of "management support" functions (operational planning systems, financial management systems, computer support programs, personnel systems, audit and evaluation programs, and the like), relatively few of which give managers much real support. In Chapter 7, we have seen how evaluation might become more useful to managers, in particular, by affecting the kinds of information that managers get on the results of their programs.

Many attempts have been made to link evaluation to budgeting, management-by-objectives, and other management support functions. There is, however, still a huge amount of work to be done in those areas.

With the passage of the Civil Service Reform Act in 1978, there was an opportunity to bring new incentives to bear on federal managers — incentives designed to stimulate demonstrable improvements in agency management and program performance. The Civil Service Reform Act was intended to create an environment in which bonuses, merit pay, and other incentives would be directed toward three objectives: providing a competent, honest, and productive work force; improving the quality of public service; and improving the efficiency, effectiveness, and responsiveness of the government to national needs.[13]

The act seemed to be a good vehicle for closer integration of management, evaluation, and personnel functions. At the suggestion of the HEW Office of Evaluation, the U.S. Office of Personnel Management asked the Department of Health, Education, and Welfare to undertake an evaluation of the impact of civil service reform on the management and performance of the Department's programs. As described in Chapter 3, this evaluation gave the Office of Evaluation the opportunity to work closely with the Assistant Secretary for Personnel Administration. The evaluation and related Office of Evaluation work focused on linkages among agency management, program management, performance planning, program evaluation, and personnel administration.

In implementing the Civil Service Reform Act, the Department was among the leaders in federal efforts to link management, program evaluation, and personnel administration in ways designed to stimulate improvements in management and program performance.

## CONCLUSION

Government organizations and organizational environments are constantly changing. There are countless opportunities for effective use of information comparing organizational performance with performance expectations. As suggested in this chapter, those in charge of evaluation can implement effective evaluation programs by setting clear evaluation objectives; by mobilizing the necessary resources; by demonstrating desired types of evaluation activities; by informally marketing their product line; and by monitoring evaluation activities and results. Whether evaluation managers are interested in management-oriented evaluation, in influencing major policy decisions, or in meeting the information needs of individual policymakers, these activities will enhance the fortunes of evaluation managers and their organizations.

Evaluation managers who are interested in management-oriented evaluation and improved agency and program performance can achieve additional impact by working closely with other management support staffs. Given the necessary resources, including the interest and support of top policymakers, evaluation managers can move even large organizations toward more effective evaluation, improved management, and improved program performance.

To the extent that top policymakers are interested in results-oriented management, therefore, evaluators can be a help. In the political and bureaucratic environment in which most policymakers and managers live, however, results-oriented management is a relatively low priority. If we are to achieve sustained progress in government management and performance, we need changes in existing incentive structures. In Chapter 9, we will examine opportunities for introduction of the needed incentives.

## NOTES TO CHAPTER 8

1. An earlier version of this chapter appears as "Management of Evaluation: Implementation of an Effective Evaluation Program," in G. Ronald Gilbert, ed., *Policy Analysis and Evaluation, Annals of Public Administration* (New York: Marcel Dekker, forthcoming). Mark Abramson, John Scanlon, and Richard Schmidt provided helpful comments in response to that earlier paper.

2. Mark A. Abramson and Joseph S. Wholey, "Organization and Management of the Evaluation Function in a Multilevel Organization," *Evaluation of Complex Systems, New Directions for Program Evaluation*, vol. 10 (San Francisco: Jossey-Bass, 1981), pp. 31–48. A somewhat similar approach is outlined in Alan P. Balutis, U.S. Department of Commerce, "Management-Oriented Evaluation" (Paper presented at the 1981 Joint Meeting of the

Evaluation Network and the Evaluation Research Society, Austin, Tex., October 1981).

3. Memorandum from Hale Champion, Under Secretary of Health, Education, and Welfare, "Guidance for Evaluation, Research, and Statistical Activities," July 28, 1978.

4. Memorandum from Hale Champion, Under Secretary of Health, Education, and Welfare, "FY 1980 Guidance for Evaluation, Research, and Statistical Activities," April 9, 1979.

5. HEW Principal Operating Components (POCs) included the Office of Human Development Services, Public Health Service, Health Care Financing Administration, Social Security Administration, and Education Division.

6. Memorandum from Nathan Stark, Under Secretary of Health, Education, and Welfare, "FY 1981 Guidance for Evaluation, Research, and Statistical Activities," February 27, 1980.

7. Abramson and Wholey, "Organization and Management," pp. 35-36.

8. Ibid., pp. 38-39.

9. Ibid., p. 44.

10. United States Senate, Committee on Appropriations, Senate Committee Report 92-247, "Departments of Labor and Health, Education, and Welfare, and Related Agencies Appropriation Bill, 1980," July 13, 1979, p. 25.

11. U.S. Department of Health, Education, and Welfare, "Evaluation Utilization in the Department of Health, Education, and Welfare" (Washington, D.C.: April 1980).

12. Letter from Patricia Roberts Harris, Secretary of Health and Human Services, to Senator Warren G. Magnuson, May 27, 1980.

13. *The Civil Service Reform Act of 1978, P.L. 95-454* (October 13, 1978).

# 9

# Creating Incentives for Improved Government Performance

## INTRODUCTION

Individual managers can achieve — and in many cases have demonstrated — efficient, effective program performance. In too few instances, however, are government managers setting clear outcome-oriented program objectives and producing demonstrably effective programs. As the size of government increases, instances of government inefficiency, ineffectiveness, and unresponsiveness increase exponentially. Existing incentives (the budget process, paths to promotion, and media attention) tend to pull policymakers and managers toward actions that inhibit rather than promote efficient, effective government. Before needed improvements in government management and performance can be achieved, changes in government incentive structures appear to be required.

In this chapter we briefly examine problems in motivating improvements in government management and performance, review the types of incentives that could be introduced, examine evidence on the effectiveness of some of the available incentives, and suggest what policymakers and staff offices can do to stimulate results-oriented management and improved agency and program performance. The discussion is intended to be suggestive rather than fully definitive. Powerful forces maintain existing modes of behavior, and new incentive schemes could produce negative consequences that could outweigh any positive accomplishments.

Sustained, creative effort is needed to produce better incentive systems and better government performance.

In the private sector, of course, incentives are routinely used to motivate improved organizational performance. Bonuses, pay raises, and "perks" like company cars and country club memberships are used to motivate improved management; incentive pay and better vacations are used to motivate improved performance in the rank-and-file.

One delightful private-sector example is that of Data Terminal Systems, a Boston-area firm manufacturing electronic cash registers that do much of the work done elsewhere by computers. To stimulate teamwork and high organizational performance in fiscal year 1977, Robert F. Collings, president of the firm, offered employees their choice of a week in London or a week at Disney World if the firm doubled both its sales and profits. By the end of the fiscal year, sales had not quite doubled, but earnings had more than doubled. The company closed its doors for a week; most employees enjoyed a week in London, but seventy-five chose the week at Disney World.[1]

In the following year Collings offered employees a "Roman Holiday" (a trip to Italy) if Data Terminal Systems could again double its sales and double its profits. By the end of fiscal year 1978, sales had doubled to $42.7 million, and profits had almost tripled, growing to $6.8 million.[2]

At Data Terminal Systems all employees were motivated to sell their company's product. Recruiting was easy; absenteeism, low; sales per employee, unusually high. Even after a blizzard, 60 percent of the employees were back on the job several days before the ban on driving was lifted. The group incentive — either all employees would be rewarded or none would be — led to peer pressure to perform well on the job.[3]

Although everything has not been rosy in the private sector (in recent years, productivity has remained constant or even declined in many sectors of the economy), most would agree that for-profit firms tend to be more efficient and effective than government organizations are. In this chapter we will inquire into the array of incentives that can be used to stimulate improved efficiency and effectiveness in government; we will see how government policymakers can create incentives needed to stimulate improved management and improved government performance.

## PROBLEMS IN ACHIEVING DEMONSTRABLE IMPROVEMENTS IN GOVERNMENT PERFORMANCE

No one believes that it will be easy to achieve demonstrable improvements in government performance. Political and bureaucratic problems, technical problems, and the possibility of negative consequences all threaten efforts to stimulate improvements in government management and performance. The problems we review here should not be minimized; fortunately, they can be overcome.

### Political and Bureaucratic Problems

In the first half of the book, we spent a good deal of time on the political problems that inhibit results-oriented management and demonstrably effective programs. In government, program goals tend to be hazy: vague, conflicting, changing, unrealistic. And there is little or no constituency for the hard job of improving government effectiveness and responsiveness. A good image counts for a great deal in government; good performance gains little currency in the media.

In the bureaucracy and among levels of government, moreover, authority is fragmented. Policymakers and policies shift all too frequently, encouraging short-term perspectives when difficult problems require long-term solutions. Program managers have too little time to do their jobs, must deal with many higher-level managers and staffs, face a bewildering multitude of checks and balances, and often have surprisingly little control over resources. In government, equity often seems more important than effectiveness, and there is an increasing accumulation of disincentives to effective management.

In his paper "A New Focus on Efficiency," James Dullea of the U.S. Office of Personnel Management characterized government's management, performance, and productivity problems as follows:

> Recently, commentators on the American private sector have criticized an emphasis on short-term profitability at the expense of long-term efficiency

and productivity. A comparable problem exists in the public sector. Reward systems must be changed if long-term performance is to be emphasized. . . . Impediments to long-term efficiency and productivity improvement include:

— A top-management focus on program and policy matters which largely excludes efficiency and long-term productivity considerations.
— Incentives to overstaff, overorganize, and overgrade.
— Few rewards for risk-taking (conformity is a safer route to career success).
— A pay system which provides executives the same salary level as many of their subordinates and an executive bonus system which rejects 80 percent of those competing.
— Punishment for not spending at the end of the fiscal year and few rewards for saving funds.[4]

Dullea proposed presidential actions to overcome these problems, including Presidential and Vice-Presidential attention; individual agency efforts to improve efficiency and productivity; establishment of performance goals and performance indicators for each federal program; establishment of a joint congressional and Executive-Branch commission to examine impediments to efficiency and productivity in the federal government and to recommend solutions; significant salary increases for federal executives; establishment of productivity reserve funds under control of individual agencies; and action to ensure that performance evaluation systems require and reward cost reduction and productivity improvement.[5]

## Technical Problems

In the preceding chapters we spent considerable time on the technical problems that inhibit effective public management and effective government performance. Given a poorly designed program or an implausible set of program objectives, managers are unlikely to demonstrate effective program performance. Public managers need to develop early warning systems that clarify program potential and allow time for alteration of program resources, program activities, or program objectives when programs are poorly designed or program objectives are unrealistic. Managers need to test ways to achieve objectives more effectively and efficiently.

Even when objectives are realistic and programs are well designed, there are technical problems in demonstrating good performance. It is often difficult to find cost-feasible measures of program performance and difficult to get timely, valid data on program performance and results. It is also difficult to communicate the complexity of program achievements in either quantitative or qualitative terms.

As we have seen in earlier chapters, the technical problems can be overcome, even in "soft" program areas like mental health. Using both quantitative and qualitative methods, managers can define organizational performance in terms of appropriate sets of objectives and performance measures; they can detect and reward good performance in subordinate units and can achieve measurable progress toward program goals.

## Possible Negative Consequences of Incentive Systems

Managers have learned to fear the negative consequences of efforts to introduce incentives intended to stimulate improved government performance. Based as they must be on a partial set of performance measures, incentive systems may distort program operations. As in the private sector, moreover, powerful incentives to achieve unrealistic objectives may lead to fraud or burnout among program managers and staff.[6] Poorly designed incentive systems may create perceptions of inequity or increase dependency on supervisors.[7]

The possibility of negative side effects cannot be eliminated if new incentive systems are to be introduced, but the possibility of these harmful side effects can be minimized. In government as in the private sector, the answers seem to be in involving many management and staff levels in establishing objectives and performance targets; in ensuring that program activities as well outcomes are assessed; and in being on the watch for negative side effects. In the public sector, moreover, there are natural opportunities to gather independent assessments from other levels of government and from interest groups, as well as opportunities to use existing data series to check on program accomplishments.

## INCENTIVES FOR IMPROVED AGENCY
## AND PROGRAM PERFORMANCE

The last word is not in on how to motivate improved government performance. In this section we briefly review the types of incentives that managers and policymakers can consider.

### To Whom Would Performance Incentives Be Directed?

Within a government organization, incentives could be directed to managers, to individual staff members, or to groups of staff members (for example, an entire branch or division). In addition, incentives could be directed to organizations themselves (using, for example, the possibility of increasing an organization's budget or renewing a grant important to an organization's survival).

### What Types of Incentives Should Be Considered?

Table 9-1 lists the types of incentives that policymakers, managers, and staff offices can consider in attempting to motivate improved organizational performance.

To be effective, incentives must be tailored to the individuals or groups to be motivated. In government, there is much evidence of the importance of intangible incentives: Personal satisfaction in a job well done, personal recognition, and public recognition are among the most important motivators. Policymakers and high-level managers can stimulate better organizational performance by giving visibility, honor, favorable publicity, increased responsibility, and more interesting assignments to those whose organizations perform well or greatly improve their performance. At least at the federal level, moreover, managers are greatly interested in two other incentives: removal of constraints and delegation of authority. There is some evidence that, in government, intangible incentive systems can stimulate much of the performance improvement that might otherwise be achieved by more costly financial incentives.[8]

"Perks" are a second class of incentives that stimulate good organizational performance. Though chauffer-driven cars and paid

**Table 9–1  Possible Incentives for Improved Agency and Program Performance**

| | *Incentives for managers and staff* | *Organizational incentives* |
|---|---|---|
| Intangible incentives | — Personal recognition (phone calls, personal notes, photographs) | |
| | — Public recognition (in speeches, newsletters, and press releases) | — Public recognition |
| | | — Support for budget proposals |
| | — Media attention | |
| | — Honor awards (certificates, citations, plaques, awards banquet) | — Honor awards |
| | — More interesting assignments | — Challenging new projects |
| | — Increased responsibility | |
| | — Removal of constraints | — Removal of constraints |
| | — Delegation of authority | — Delegation of authority |
| "Perks" | — Travel to conferences | |
| | — Selection for training programs | |
| | — Educational leave | |
| | — More flexible working hours | |
| | — Better office space | |
| | — Free parking | |
| | — Additional annual leave, sabbaticals | |
| Financial incentives | — Promotions | — Increases in program budgets |
| | — Bonuses | — Allocation of discretionary funds |
| | — Cash awards | — Discretionary use of savings |
| | — Pay raises | — Staff allocations |
| | | — Allocation of overhead resources |
| | | — Renewal of discretionary grants |

club memberships are rare in government, government can reward high-performing individuals with transfers to more desirable locations, better office space, free parking, educational leave, or more flexible working hours. In Canada additional annual leave is used to reward high-performing managers.

Finally, financial incentives continue to be powerful motivators for individuals and for organizations as well. Promotions, bonuses, and pay raises can be used to stimulate good individual performance; group awards can be given to entire units.

Budget and staff allocations are the most powerful incentives for government organizations, since they represent life itself. Though the major budget and staffing decisions are made on other grounds, modest increments of staff or discretionary funds could appropriately be used to stimulate and reward more effective organizational performance. And, though there are all sorts of problems to be overcome, in many instances renewal of discretionary grants could be conditioned on organizational performance.

## What About Disincentives for Poor Performance?

Frederick Mosher reminds us that disincentives have traditionally been used to penalize fraud, inefficiency, or ineffectiveness. Among these disincentives have been death, removal or replacement, demotion, elimination or reduction of authority, elimination or reduction of resources, reprimands, and unfavorable publicity.[9]

Why are we not paying more attention to the use of disincentives? It is partly a matter of taste, partly a matter of exposition, and partly a recognition of reality. I am, I admit, a positive-incentives person. Furthermore, when one is allocating a fixed resource, awarding incentives to some effectively imposes disincentives on others by depriving the others of resources that might have been theirs.

More important is the fact that, when authority is divided or the way to effective performance is uncertain, it may be counterproductive to penalize managers or organizations whose performance is below expected levels. Instead, we can reward high performers with additional resources and honors — and threaten poor performers with training and technical assistance. In most government programs, we would consider removing resources from poor performers only as a last resort.

## How Can We Learn More About This Area?

In the area of incentive systems as in public management itself, we need to learn more about production of effective programs. The results-oriented management scale (Chapter 1, Table 1-1) gives us a tool for monitoring the performance of programs and agencies. (As we noted in Chapter 3, this scale is being used in evaluating the impact of civil service reform on the management and performance of programs in the U.S. Department of Health and Human Services.) Not only can we do case studies of high performers to learn what went right, we can also do case studies of poor performers to learn what went wrong.

Utilizing time series data generated by use of the results-oriented management scale, moreover, we will be in position to undertake experimental or quasi-experimental demonstration projects (Chapter 5) to learn whether specific incentive systems stimulate results-oriented management and improved program performance.

## INCENTIVES FOR MANAGERS AND STAFF

In their paper for the 1979 Public Management Research Conference, Lyman Porter and James Perry reviewed what was then known about employee motivation. They noted the absence of accepted theory and the absence of clear prescriptions in the area of employee motivation. In the public sector, they cited the National Commission on Productivity finding that merit pay raises have not proven to be particularly effective.[10] They noted the difficulties in designing equitable formulas tying monetary incentives to performance, and the fact that goal-setting (and feedback on performance) appears to produce performance improvements. Porter and Perry concluded that goal-setting is an attractive alternative to financial incentive systems in the public sector.[11]

In their book *Productivity and Motivation,* John Greiner and his colleagues reviewed state and local government initiatives, including use of monetary incentives, performance targeting, employee performance appraisal systems, and job enrichment programs.[12] Greiner and his colleagues reached the following conclusions: (1) Given a clear set of objectives and appropriate performance measures, monetary incentives for state and local government employees have produced significant improvements in efficiency and cost savings. (2) In the private sector, performance targeting (goal-setting) appears to have led to improved employee performance. (3) There is little evidence available on the effectiveness of performance targeting in the public sector. (4) Standard "merit pay" systems are unlikely to achieve improvements in performance. (5) There is little evidence available on the effectiveness of target-based performance appraisals. (6) A number of job enrichment approaches have led to improvements in efficiency or effectiveness.[13]

When the Civil Service Reform Act was being implemented in the federal government, Richard Stimson reviewed the literature, concluding that the motivational effects of money on management productivity were far from clear except when large lump-sum payments are made.[14]

Leibenstein offers some interesting speculations as to reasons why managers of private firms often fail to take advantage of available knowledge to improve productivity and profits. Just as in the public sector, it appears that managers of private firms are often busy with other matters.[15]

At this time, it appears that we still have to work from individual instances in hypothesizing the effects of incentive systems. Though the research cited above yields mixed results, the following examples indicate that incentive systems can have positive effects on program and agency performance.

## Intangible Incentives

In Chapter 1 we examined the results achieved at the Harlem Valley Psychiatric Center, where Dr. Yoosuf Haveliwala used a wide variety of intangible incentives to stimulate improved individual and organizational performance.

Following his mentor, President Lyndon Johnson, a master of motivation and persuasion,[16] Secretary Joseph A. Califano, Jr., used the incentives and disincentives of his personal attention to stimulate the setting of ambitious program performance targets and the achievement of demonstrable improvements in the management and performance of Department of Health, Education, and Welfare programs (see Chapters 1 and 7).

When a department-wide performance improvement initiative was proposed to him in 1979, Nathan Stark, then Under Secretary of Health, Education, and Welfare, immediately responded with examples from his private-sector experience, where industrial plants had moved from very poor to very good safety records and hospitals had improved their efficiency when employees were made aware of realistic objectives and were given periodic reports on the organizations' progress toward those objectives.[17]

In the present condition of the federal bureaucracy, which is bound up by a multiplicity of checks and balances, I am impressed with the value of removal of constraints and of delegation of authority as incentives for federal managers. Federal managers respond very well to the proposal that removal of constraints and delegation of authority would be effective incentives.[18] Given such authority, NASA did land a man on the moon. In my more modest experience, I saw how delegation of authority led Department of Health, Education, and Welfare agencies to move toward management-oriented evaluation.[19]

## Financial Incentives

Even before implementation of the Civil Service Reform Act, the federal government had an Incentive Awards program that a number of agencies had used to achieve improved organizational performance. In the Department of Defense, for example, the General Accounting Office reports the following accomplishments:

Low productivity, leave abuse, high turnover, and low morale among data transcribers were a serious problem at a West Coast naval shipyard. In an endeavor to correct the problem areas, Navy research specialists were called upon in 1976 to develop an awards program.

Working with shipyard managers, the research specialists set the specific goals of the program to increase individual employee output and reduce overtime and work backlog. In designing the program, Navy officials interviewed employees to determine (1) if they perceived themselves capable of increasing performance if meaningful incentives were available and (2) what types of awards would be an incentive to improve performance. Performance standards and performance measurement systems were then developed which identified individual performance achieved in terms of quantity and quality. This measurement system enabled the Navy to identify and reward employees whose individual performance exceeded normal expectations.

The amount of an award is determined on a weekly basis by comparing the employee's actual performance to the standard. The award amount is equal to 11 percent of the cost savings and is paid the employee by a monthly check separate from the normal payroll check.

During the first year the new incentive program was used, productivity increased 18 percent. In addition, overtime requirements, which had previously averaged 54 hours per week, were virtually eliminated and a significant work backlog was eliminated. Because of the improvements at the first shipyard, the program was implemented at another West Coast shipyard with the same positive results. The Navy is currently trying to implement a similar program for all installations employing data transcribers.[20]

In 1981 San Diego completed construction of the Tijuana Trolley, the first "light rail" transit line built in the United States in the last twenty years. Transit officials attributed a good deal of their success in completing the project on time and within budget to their linking employee salaries to budgets and schedules.[21]

And part of the formula for HEW's success in gaining control of the Guaranteed Student Loan Program was a system of incentive awards for employees who got large numbers of defaulted loans back into repayment status (see Chapter 1).

The biggest current effort to use financial incentives to motivate public managers is in federal implementation of the Civil Service Reform Act, which provides potential bonuses for thousands of career senior executives and merit pay tied to performance for tens of thousands of middle managers. As suggested in Chapter 3, the Civil Service Reform Act has the potential for positive impact on the performance and results of government organizations. With the jury still out and many problems already apparent, my personal hope is that this legislation will eventually be made to work.

## ORGANIZATIONAL INCENTIVES

In Chapter 1 we noted Peter Drucker's observation that government organizations are radically different from for-profit firms because government organizations are paid out of budget allocations rather than being paid for satisfying taxpayers or customers by producing results. In government organizations the budget is the major incentive, affecting the behavior of management all year, every year. Drucker noted that the budget process causes government organizations to fragment their activities, trying to please everyone who might affect their budgets.

In this and the following section we examine what has been done — and what could be done — to introduce organizational incentives that will stimulate and reward improved management and performance in government organizations.

## Intangible Incentives for Government Organizations

In the public sector as in our own lives, we can go a long way on personal satisfaction and recognition for a job well done.[22] For many years I have advocated that, in the absence of other organizational incentives, policymakers and high-level managers should at least recognize jobs well done at an annual "Awards Banquet." I envisioned a public school system, for example, bound up in civil service restrictions and union agreements, yet still finding a way to recognize excellent organizational performance by honoring the principals, teachers, and staff of those schools which had performed best, given the environments and student populations with which they had to deal.

In the Department of Health and Human Services, I was pleased to find a small agency, the Office of Child Support Enforcement, that has publicly recognized good performance at such ceremonies. The Office of Child Support Enforcement works through federally funded state agencies to get absent parents to contribute to the support of their children, many of whom are on welfare. The Office of Child Support Enforcement tracks the performance of each state's child support enforcement agency on several success indicators (for example, child support payments collected); recognizes high performers on selected indicators in their newsletter; and has held awards ceremonies honoring states with outstanding performance.[23] The authorizing legislation also provides strong financial incentives that encourage improved state performance and encourage cooperation among states. Over the last several years the Child Support Enforcement program has become increasingly efficient and increasingly effective.[24]

## Financial Incentives for Government Organizations

We noted earlier that HEW's Bureau of Community Health Services stimulated improved regional and grantee performance by allocating staff and grant funds on the basis of their assessment of regional and grantee performance on priority output indicators (see Chapter 1).

For many years, the U.S. Employment Service has allocated grant funds (which pay for the staffing of state and local employment security agencies) under a system designed to stimulate state agency performance in achieving national objectives. Funds are allocated to state agencies on the basis of a formula that includes: (1) their past productivity in placing job applicants; (2) improvements in productivity; (3) job placement of veterans, unemployment insurance recipients, and minorities; and (4) the level and expected duration of the jobs filled. The allocation formula is adjusted periodically to better reflect national priorities and state agency accomplishments.[25]

Many government agencies encourage efficiency and cost savings by allowing subordinate units to keep — and reallocate — a portion of savings achieved in a given fiscal year. Here is an example from a General Accounting Office report:

> This latter incentive has been successfully used by the Internal Revenue Service. They call it profit sharing and use the technique with their regional managers. . . . If a manager improves his or her organization's productivity over a period of a year, he or she is given back resources equal to about one-half of the annual savings. The manager can use these resources as he or she deems appropriate.[26]

In a similar scheme designed to achieve economies in the use of fuel, the U.S. Air Force began to track fuel expenditures at each base, and then established a system that allowed each air base to keep and reallocate 100 percent of any dollar savings on fuel. In the following year, lower target levels would be set.[27] In the Internal Revenue Service, regional managers keep 50 percent of the savings on an ongoing basis; in the Air Force, base commanders keep 100 percent of the savings on a one-time basis.

## WHAT CAN POLICYMAKERS AND STAFF OFFICES DO TO CREATE NEEDED INCENTIVES?

If our analysis is correct, improvements in government performance and public confidence in government depend to some extent on results-oriented management and effective performance at agency, bureau, program, and operating levels. But managers will manage as they have always managed, responding to the incentives in their environments. Here we examine what policy-makers and staff offices can do to create changes in management environments that will encourage managers to produce demonstrably effective programs.

## What Policymakers Can Do

According to the Constitution, a major responsibility of the President is to "take Care that the Laws be faithfully executed."[28] Presidents, other chief executives, and agency heads regularly express their strong support for efficient, effective government that responds to public needs. But what can policymakers actually do to stimulate better government performance?

In addition to encouraging good people to serve in government, policymakers affect government performance by the issues on which they focus attention and by the policies that they adopt. Policymakers control or influence major overhead resources that can be used to stimulate improved management and improved agency and program performance.

A government-wide or agency-wide effort to stimulate demonstrable improvements in program performance requires some system for identifying and rewarding effective and improved program performance. Such a system needs to track the progress of agency programs in achieving improved performance, and it should set in motion appropriate rewards for achieving higher levels of performance:

— Level 1: Policy and management agreement on an appropriate set of program objectives and performance indicators. (*Reward follows.*)
— Level 2: Establishment of an appropriate system for assessing program performance in terms of the agreed-on objectives and performance indicators. (*Reward follows.*)
— Level 3: Policy and management agreement on realistic target levels of expected or improved program performance. (*Reward follows.*)

— Level 4: Management establishment of a system for using program performance information to stimulate improved program performance. (*Reward follows.*)
— Level 5: Achievement of acceptable program performance in terms of the agreed-on performance targets. (*Reward follows.*)

Here the rewards would be incentives like those listed in Table 9-1. Some could be granted by staff offices; others (for example, personal recognition, delegation of authority, support for budget requests, authority to maintain or increase numbers of staff, award of bonuses) would often require action by the chief executive, the agency head, or a principal deputy. A system for verifying and rewarding results-oriented management and effective program performance would require the chief executive's or agency head's agreement on the incentives to be used and on the criteria for awarding the incentives. Operation of the system would require management conferences (among policymakers, line managers, and participating staff offices) to reach agreement on program objectives, performance indicators, and performance targets, and to review evidence on program accomplishments.[29]

Coordination would be important. The idea would be to harness the government's (or agency's) overhead functions to create appropriate incentives. To stimulate more effective performance in a challenging, high-priority program area, for example, policymakers might use some or all of the following incentives: loosening of constraints (such as giving the manager the ability to hire his or her own people, without policy-level clearances), delegation of authority, authority to maintain or increase number of staff, public recognition, media attention, and allocation of bonuses and funds for merit pay raises.

## What Central Management Groups Can Do

With the active support or at least the approval of the chief executive or agency head, a central management unit (for example, the Office of Management and Budget or an agency Office of Administration) could annually rate agency programs in terms of their progress in results-oriented management (see Tables 1-1 and 1-4). High performers could then be recognized and rewarded; low performers would be encouraged to do better.

Though not using the results-oriented management scale (which makes inter-program comparisons more feasible), Laurence Silberman made a related proposal in 1978: To encourage reexamination of federal programs and elimination of those that are least effective, Silberman suggested that each year the President be required to rank the programs in each agency in terms of their relative effectiveness (compared to other programs in the same agency) and then to explain the basis of his ranking. Silberman suggested that at least the following criteria be used in the ranking process: (1) coherence of statutory objectives, (2) design of the program, (3) quality of management.[30] Silberman's criteria relate well to the evaluability/manageability criteria (Chapters 2 and 3) and to the levels on the results-oriented management scale (Chapter 1, Table 1-1).

## What Budget Offices Can Do

Budget power is real power. If the budget and appropriations processes were used to reward results-oriented management and demonstrably effective programs, this would be the greatest incentive of all.

Though most budget decisions will continue to be made on other grounds (fiscal constraints, relative need, and political power will always be important), it appears feasible to use the budget process to add relatively small amounts of discretionary funds to well-managed programs. Since discretion is highly valued by managers, even small increases in discretionary funds would represent important incentives.

At a minimum, demonstrably effective programs could be protected in budget-cutting exercises.

## What Personnel Offices Can Do

Personnel offices could ensure that, in the award of bonuses and merit pay to line managers, heavy weight would be given to demonstrated progress in results-oriented management and achievement of effective or greatly improved program performance. In the federal government, for example, the largest Senior Executive Service bonuses (the presidential $10,000 and $20,000 awards) could and should go primarily to line managers who have demonstrated significant progress in producing effective or greatly improved programs terms of agreed-on program objectives, performance indicators, and performance targets.

Personnel offices could also sponsor experimental changes in agency personnel systems, to test the effects of such changes on agency and program management and performance. Though the Civil Service Reform Act provides the U.S. Office of Personnel Management with such authority, that authority has not been used to any great extent.

## What Inspectors General, Auditors, and Evaluators Can Do

The General Accounting Office, Inspectors General, and audit agencies are well situated to perform the key function of rating the progress of each agency program on the results-oriented management scale (Chapter 1, Table 1-1) and publicizing the results. Independent evaluation offices (and oversight committees) could perform a similar function.

My own preference is that agency evaluation offices put most of their efforts into helping move programs along the results-oriented management scale, carrying out the management-oriented evaluation activities discussed in earlier chapters. As in my own experience in the Department of Health and Human Services, however, it may be necessary for evaluation offices to provide at least some of the resources for objective assessment of agency progress in results-oriented management.

## What Public Affairs Offices Can Do

Since media attention is very important in government, public affairs offices are potentially important to results-oriented management. Two important public affairs functions might be (1) publicizing a chief executive's or agency head's interest in and concern with demonstrable improvements in program performance and results, and (2) publicizing managers' success in moving toward improved program performance (better services for the public or savings for the taxpayer). To enhance the credibility of press releases, outside audits might be required.

## CONCLUSION

Many incentive systems have been implemented in government. A much smaller number of incentive systems have been associated with improvements in the efficiency, effectiveness, and responsiveness of government organizations.

Many incentive schemes are costly, either in dollars or in production of undesirable side effects. In the absence of appropriate incentives, however, public organizations often tend to promote the private interests of managers and staff rather than the public interests for which they were created.

In this chapter we outlined a few of the many possibilities open to government managers and policymakers who wish to stimulate improvements in the performance of organizations for which they are responsible. Some of these incentive systems could also be used by public-interest groups to stimulate better performance in relevant public agencies and programs.

At this point, readers are asked to explore opportunities for introducing appropriate organizational incentive systems into environments over which they have some degree of influence. Although the way to better government is often hard to find, appropriate incentive systems can help guide organizations along the right paths.

## NOTES TO CHAPTER 9

1. Steven Solomon, "How a Whole Company Earned Itself a Roman Holiday," *Fortune,* vol. 99 (January 15, 1979), pp. 80–83.

2. Ibid., p. 82.

3. Ibid., p. 83.

4. James F. Dullea, "A New Focus on Efficiency: Executive Summary" (Washington, D.C.: U.S. Office of Management and Budget, January 16, 1981), p. 1.

5. Ibid., pp. 1–2.

6. George Getschow, "Overdriven Execs: Some Middle Managers Cut

Corners to Achieve High Corporate Goals," *Wall Street Journal,* November 8, 1979, pp. 1 and 19.

7. Michael Maccoby, "Motivating the Civil Service," *Washington Post,* May 20, 1978, Op-ed page.

8. Lyman W. Porter and James L. Perry, Graduate School of Administration, University of California (Irvine), "Motivation and Public Management: Concepts, Issues, and Research Needs" (Paper presented at the Public Management Research Conference, The Brookings Institution, Washington, D.C., November 19, 1979).

9. Frederick C. Mosher, *The GAO: The Quest for Accountability in American Government* (Boulder, Colo.: Westview Press, 1979), p. 235.

10. Porter and Perry, "Motivation and Public Management," p. 42.

11. Ibid., p. 45.

12. John M. Greiner and others, *Productivity and Motivation: A Review of State and Local Government Initiatives* (Washington, D.C.: The Urban Institute Press, 1981).

13. Ibid., pp. 112, 150, 216–217, and 399–403.

14. Richard A. Stimson, "Performance Pay: Will It Work?" *The Bureaucrat,* Summer 1980, pp. 39–47.

15. Harvey Leibenstein, "Allocative Efficiency and 'X-Efficiency,' " *American Economic Review,* vol. 56, no. 3 (1966) pp. 392–415.

16. See Doris Kearns, *Lyndon Johnson and the American Dream* (New York: Harper and Row, 1976).

17. Meeting on the HEW Performance Improvement Initiative, December 13, 1979.

18. See, for example, Charles F. Bingman and Frank P. Sherwood, eds., *Management Improvement Agenda for the Eighties* (Charlottesville, Va.: U.S. Office of Personnel Management, Federal Executive Institute, FEI B-26, 1981).

19. The Department delegated approval of evaluability assessments costing less than $100,000 to agency level (two levels below Department level).

20. Comptroller General of the United States, *Does the Federal Incentive Awards Program Improve Productivity?* (Washington, D.C.: U.S. General Accounting Office, FGMSD-79-9, 1979), pp. 7–8.

21. See Jerry Schneider, "Clang, Clang Goes the Trolley! And the Sound Means Mass Transit Savings," *Washington Post,* September 7, 1980, pp. F1 and F7; and "Trolley System Saves Dollars for San Diego," *Public Administration Times,* July 15, 1981, p. 1.

22. See John W. Gardner, *Self-Renewal* (New York: Harper and Row, 1964).

23. Meetings with Office of Child Support Enforcement staff, 1980.

24. See Chapter 7.

25. See *Guide for Applying the Resource Allocation Formula to Measure Employment Service Performance and to Allocate Title III ES Grants to the States for Fiscal Year 1977* (Washington, D.C.: U.S. Department of Labor, United States Employment and Training Administration, Handbook No. 340, 1976).

26. Comptroller General, *Does the Federal Incentive Awards Program Improve Productivity?*, p. 22.

27. Richard A. Stubbing, U.S. Office of Management and Budget, "Incentives" (Lecture at the University of Southern California's Washington Public Affairs Center, Washington, D.C., January 15, 1981).

28. Constitution of the United States, Article II, Section 3.

29. John Scanlon suggested development of such a system (personal communication, 1978).

30. Laurence H. Silberman, "If Not the Best, At Least Not the Worst," *Commonsense*, vol. 1, no. 1 (Summer 1978), pp. 18–26.

# 10

## Evaluation and Effective Government: Future Prospects

This book developed from the conviction that government policy-makers, managers, and staff can and should act to produce demonstrable improvements in government management, performance, and results, and thus help restore public confidence in government. In this chapter we recapitulate our central argument, examine evidence supporting the argument and some of the problems that hinder progress in the desired direction, and explore the prospects of achieving demonstrable improvements in government performance.[1]

## THE CENTRAL ARGUMENT

Our central argument proceeds along the following lines:

### Assumptions

1. Government can perform effectively and can demonstrate the value of program activities.
2. Government often fails to perform as efficiently and effectively as it should, or fails to demonstrate the value of program activities to policymakers and to the public.
3. Public perceptions of government are often negative, either be-

cause government performance is poor or because good performance is not communicated, rewarded, and reinforced.

4. We need demonstrable improvements in government management, performance, and results.

5. Demonstrably efficient, demonstrably effective government programs can be produced by carrying through the results-oriented management steps outlined in Chapter 1, demonstrating the value of program activities to policymakers and to the public. The necessary results-oriented management activities include getting policy and management agreement on the most important results to be achieved by government programs, establishing systems for documenting the extent to which program performance and results are acceptable, achieving acceptable program performance and results, and communicating program performance and results to policymakers and to the public.

6. Sufficient technology is available to allow production of demonstrably effective programs.

7. All that is needed is the will to make it happen.

## Conclusions

1. Government policymakers, managers, and staff organizations should take responsibility for results: production of demonstrably effective programs.

2. Government managers and policymakers should place priority on, and devote available staff and overhead resources to, results-oriented management activities that will produce demonstrably effective programs.

3. Staff organizations and analysts should place priority on management-oriented evaluation activities that will achieve demonstrable improvements in government management, performance, and results. These management-oriented evaluation activities include working with program managers and policymakers to identify important program objectives and program performance indicators, developing systems for assessing program performance and results, developing systems for using program-performance information to improve program perfor-

mance, and communicating program performance and results to policymakers and to the public.

## THE EVIDENCE

In our first chapter, we began with definitions of "results-oriented management" and "demonstrably effective program," and saw why demonstrable improvements are needed in the performance and results of government programs. We then examined several examples of results-oriented management that led to demonstrably effective performance in the Bureau of Community Health Services, in the Guaranteed Student Loan Program, in the Harlem Valley Psychiatric Center, and in the Sunnyvale city government. In Chapters 7 and 9, we encountered several more examples of results-oriented management, in the Department of Health, Education, and Welfare, in the Department of Defense, and in the Internal Revenue Service.

Throughout the book we have explored both a general strategy and specific approaches that can be used to achieve results-oriented management and demonstrably effective performance in government programs and agencies. In Chapters 2-4 we saw how evaluability assessment could help managers and policymakers come to consensus on sets of realistic program objectives, needed changes in program activities, and needed changes in collection and use of information on program performance. In Chapters 5-7 we explored ways in which managers and policymakers could quickly get usable information on the outcomes of program activities, including early warning of emerging problems. Because the more "researchy" evaluation designs often are unfeasible or too costly, we suggested evaluation approaches more appropriate to the environments in which public managers operate. Finally, in Chapters 8 and 9, we moved from individual program management and evaluation issues to systems designed to achieve better management and performance throughout an entire agency or an entire unit of government. A number of promising incentive systems were identified, including the use of goal-setting (setting clear objectives and providing continual feedback on program performance and results), relaxation of constraints and delegation of authority, and the sharing of 50 percent of savings with those organizations which achieve the savings.

## PROBLEMS AND SOLUTIONS

Policymakers, managers, and staff are busy with thousands of day-to-day problems. There is little or no public demand or support for efforts to improve government management and performance, unless the "management improvements" are directly tied to tax-rate reductions. The media are much more interested in one bad apple than in a bushel of good ones. There are problems in getting agreement on what "good performance" means in government programs and agencies, problems in getting information on program and agency performance and results, and problems in motivating improved program and agency performance. Is it possible, then, to achieve and demonstrate systematic improvements in government management, performance, and results? Or will excellent government management and performance remain rare events?

Given what we now know, it seems fair to expect the managers of any given program to be able, within a year, to move the program to Level 1 on the results-oriented management scale: getting policy and management agreement on a set of outcome-oriented program objectives and program performance indicators in terms of which the program will be assessed and managed.[2] In many cases, they will also be able to move the program to Level 2 (establishment of a system for assessing program performance and results in terms of the agreed-on program objectives and program performance indicators) within the first year. In any event, by the end of a second year, it seems fair to expect program and agency managers to have moved the program to Levels 3 and 4: establishment of realistic target levels of expected program performance and results, and establishment of systems for using program-performance information to improve program performance and results. By the end of a third year, it seems fair to expect program and agency managers to have moved the program to Levels 5 and 6: achievement of efficient, effective program performance, and communication of program performance and results to policymakers and to the public. Many programs should be able to move more rapidly along the results-oriented management scale.

In any large agency or unit of government, however, there will be huge numbers of programs and subprograms, each of which is a potential candidate for demonstrable improvement. How can higher-level managers, policymakers, and staff organizations stimulate improved performance and results across these large bureaucracies?

To achieve demonstrably effective performance in most or all of the important programs in a large agency or in an entire unit of government, higher-level managers, policymakers, and staff organizations must find ways to enlist the cooperation of line managers. A successful strategy will almost certainly include the introduction of new incentives to gain the cooperation and support of line managers and their organizations. Tangible incentives might include authority for program or agency managers to keep and reallocate 50 percent of any savings achieved, authority to consolidate activities and reallocate staff, authority to install systems of bonuses or to grant temporary or permanent promotions and pay raises, protection from budget cuts, and support for managers' budget and legislative proposals. Intangible incentives might include personal recognition, public recognition, increased responsibility, removal of constraints, and delegation of authority.

Given a clear definition of the task to be accomplished (production of demonstrable improvements in program performance and results) and given the appropriate incentives, many managers will be able to progress along the results-oriented management scale using their own resources. In other cases, analytical staff support may be needed to assist managers in identifying appropriate program objectives and performance indicators, to assist in developing systems for monitoring program performance and results, or to assist in demonstrating the value of program activities to policymakers or to the public. In Chapters 2-5, we saw the usefulness of evaluability assessment and rapid-feedback evaluation in identifying program objectives and developing systems for assessing program performance and results. In a number of other cases, simplified zero-base budgeting processes have been used to identify high-priority program objectives and performance indicators.[3]

In times of limited resources and diminished public confidence in government, the challenge of the 1980s is to extend demonstrably effective performance to entire agencies. In recent years, I have been encouraged to find a number of examples of efforts to achieve and demonstrate government-wide or agency-wide performance improvements: in local governments like Sunnyvale, California, in state-level governments like the Province of Ontario and the Commonwealth of Virginia,[4] and at federal level in the U.S. Department of Health, Education, and Welfare (now the Department of Health and Human Services).

The combined efforts of public administrators, academic institutions, and public interest groups will be needed to develop management policies (goals, objectives, standards) and working models that will guide line managers and staff organizations toward activities that will improve the performance and results of government programs and agencies. Over the next several years, I intend to put a good deal of my own efforts into helping develop management policies and working models that will assist government policymakers, managers, and staff organizations in achieving and demonstrating improved government performance and results.

## CONCLUSION

Our goal is good government. "Good government" used to mean not stealing money and not filling public payrolls with political hacks. Today, the term means much more: it now means producing public services that efficiently and effectively respond to the needs of an increasingly complex, increasingly interrelated society.

In the 1980s and beyond, evaluation resources are likely to be diminished, while the needs of government managers, policymakers, and the public are likely to grow. Managers will need help in sorting through the conflicting and often unrealistic expectations of policymakers and higher-level executives. Policymakers will need help in determining whether agency and program activities are achieving satisfactory results, and help in spotting important negative consequences of government interventions. Members of the public will need effective government services, while the general public will continue to demand that taxes and public expenditures be controlled. In the absence of information demonstrating that public services are effective, the general public will increasingly question maintaining those services.

Evaluators will have to produce more relevant, less expensive evaluations if evaluators are to have roles in the constrained resource environments of the 1980s and beyond. As we have seen, approaches are available through which policymakers, managers, and analysts can achieve and demonstrate better government performance  and results. Outsiders who wish to stimulate better government performance can also use many of these approaches. These approaches and methods have been developed and tested in political and bureaucratic settings at federal, state, and local levels. In these pages we have explored approaches that can lead, and have led, to better government.

We need better government and greater public confidence in government. The leadership challenges of the 1980s are great, but they can and must be met. In the 1980s and in the remainder of this century, the product line of government policymakers, managers, and staff organizations must be demonstrably effective programs and agencies: government programs and agencies that are demonstrably efficient, demonstrably effective, and demonstrably responsive to public needs. For all of us, inside and outside government, it's time to get back to work!

## NOTES TO CHAPTER 10

1. John Scanlon and James Bell provided helpful comments on an earlier version of this chapter.

2. References to Level 1, Level 2, and so on, are to the results-oriented management scale introduced in Chapter 1, Table 1-1.

3. See Joseph S. Wholey, *Zero-Base Budgeting and Program Evaluation* (Lexington, Mass.: D. C. Heath, 1978).

4. The Province of Ontario has used a system of Managing By Results (MBR) for several years. See "Managing the 80s: A Report of the Management Board of Cabinet for 1980–81" (Toronto, Ontario: Province of Ontario, Management Board Secretariat, July 1981).

In 1982, the Commonwealth of Virginia initiated a series of management and evaluation initiatives designed to produce demonstrable improvements in the efficiency and effectiveness of state government. See Charles S. Robb, Governor of Virginia, "Remarks at the Agency Head Luncheon" (Richmond, Virginia: May 3, 1982) and "Agency Head Briefing" (Richmond, Virginia: June 9, 1982).

# Selected Bibliography

Abramson, Mark A., and others. "Evaluating a Personnel System." *Review of Public Personnel Administration* (forthcoming).

—— and Joseph S. Wholey. "Organization and Management of the Evaluation Function in a Multilevel Organization." *Evaluation of Complex Systems: New Directions for Program Evaluation*, vol. 10. San Francisco: Jossey-Bass, 1981, pp. 31–48.

Anthony, Robert N., and Regina E. Herzlinger. *Management Control in Non-profit Organizations*. Homewood, Ill.: Richard D. Irwin, 1975.

Bingman, Charles F., and Frank P. Sherwood, eds. *Management Improvement Agenda for the Eighties*. Charlottesville, Va.: U.S. Office of Personnel Management, Federal Executive Institute, FEI B-26, 1981.

Campbell, Donald T. "Reforms as Experiments." *American Psychologist*, vol. 24 (1969), pp. 409–429.

—— and Julian C. Stanley. *Experimental and Quasi-Experimental Designs for Research*. Chicago: Rand McNally, 1966.

Cook, Thomas D., and Donald T. Campbell. *Quasi-Experimentation: Design and Analysis Issues for Field Settings*. Chicago: Rand McNally College Publishing Company, 1979.

——and Charles S. Reichardt. *Qualitative and Quantitative Methods in Evaluation Research*. Beverly Hills, Calif.: Sage Publications, 1979.

Cronbach, Lee J., and others. *Toward Reform of Program Evaluation*. San Francisco: Jossey-Bass, 1980.

Drucker, Peter F. *Management: Tasks, Responsibilities, Practices*. New York: Harper and Row, 1974.

Dullea, James F., U.S. Office of Personnel Management. "A New Focus on Efficiency." Washington, D.C., January 16, 1981.

Greiner, John M., and others. *Productivity and Motivation: A Review of State and Local Government Initiatives.* Washington, D.C.: The Urban Institute Press, 1981.

Hatry, Harry P., Richard E. Winnie, and Donald M. Fisk. *Practical Program Evaluation for State and Local Governments.* 2nd ed. Washington, D.C.: The Urban Institute Press, 1981.

Hendricks, Michael. "Qualitative Evaluation at the Cabinet Level." In N. L. Smith, ed., *Federal Efforts to Develop New Evaluation Methods, New Directions for Program Evaluation,* no. 12 (San Francisco: Jossey-Bass, 1981), pp. 5-24.

Hochstim, Joseph R. "A Critical Comparison of Three Strategies of Collecting Data from Households." *American Statistical Association Journal,* vol. 62, no. 319 (September 1967), pp. 976-989.

Horst, Pamela, and others. "Program Management and the Federal Evaluator." *Public Administration Review,* vol. 34, no. 4 (July/August 1974), pp. 300-308.

Isaac, Stephen, and William B. Michael. *Handbook in Research and Evaluation.* 2nd ed. San Diego, Calif.: EdITS Publishers, 1981.

Levine, Murray. *From State Hospital to Psychiatric Center.* Lexington, Mass.: D. C. Heath, 1980.

Millar, Rhona, and others. *Developing Client Outcome Monitoring Systems: A Guide for State and Local Social Services Agencies.* Washington, D.C.: The Urban Institute, 1981.

Mosher, Frederick C. *The GAO: The Quest for Accountability in American Government.* Boulder, Colo.: Westview Press, 1979.

Nay, Joe N. and Peg Kay. *Government Oversight and Evaluability Assessment.* Lexington, Mass.: D. C. Heath, 1982.

Patton, Michael Quinn. *Creative Evaluation.* Beverly Hills, Calif.: Sage Publications, 1981.

—— *Qualitive Evaluation Methods.* Beverly Hills, Calif.: Sage Publications, 1980.

—— *Utilization-Focused Evaluation.* Beverly Hills, Calif.: Sage Publications, 1978.

Pressman, Jeffrey L., and Aaron B. Wildavsky. *Implementation.* Berkeley, Calif.: University of California Press, 1973.

Riecken, Henry W., and Robert F. Boruch, eds. *Social Experimentation: A Method for Planning and Evaluating Social Intervention.* New York: Academic Press, 1974.

Rivlin, Alice M. *Systematic Thinking for Social Action.* Washington, D.C.: The Brookings Institution, 1971.

—— and P. Michael Timpane, eds. *Planned Variation in Education*. Washington, D.C.: The Brookings Institution, 1975.

Rutman, Leonard, ed. *Evaluation Research Methods: A Basic Guide*. Beverly Hills, Calif.: Sage Publications, 1977.

—— *Planning Useful Evaluations: Evaluability Assessment*. Beverly Hills, Calif.: Sage Publications, 1980.

Schainblatt, Alfred H., and Harry P. Hatry. *Mental Health Services: What Happens to the Clients?* Washington, D.C.: The Urban Institute, 1979.

Schmidt, Richard E., John W. Scanlon, and James B. Bell. *Evaluability Assessment: Making Public Programs Work Better*. Rockville, Md.: U.S. Department of Health, Education, and Welfare, Project Share, Human Services Monograph No. 14, 1979.

Silberman, Laurence H. "If Not the Best, At Least Not the Worst." *Commonsense*, vol. 1, no. 1 (Summer 1978), pp. 18–26.

Stone, Eugene. *Research Methods in Organizational Behavior*. Glenview, Ill.: Scott, Foresman, 1978.

Tuchfarber, Alfred J., and William R. Klecka. *Random Digit Dialing*. Washington, D.C.: Police Foundation, 1976.

Weiss, Carol H. *Evaluation Research: Methods of Assessing Program Effectiveness*. Englewood Cliffs, N.J.: Prentice-Hall, 1972.

—— ed. *Using Social Research in Public Policy Making*. Lexington, Mass.: D. C. Heath, 1977.

Wholey, Joseph S. *Evaluation: Promise and Performance*. Washington, D.C.: The Urban Institute, 1979.

—— *Zero-Base Budgeting and Program Evaluation*. Lexington, Mass.: D. C. Heath, 1978.

—— and others. *Federal Evaluation Policy*. Washington, D.C.: The Urban Institute, 1970.

Wildavsky, Aaron B. *Speaking Truth to Power: The Art and Craft of Policy Analysis*. Boston: Little, Brown, 1979.

# Index

About the Author

Joseph S. Wholey (Ph.D., Philosophy, M.A., Mathematics, Harvard) is a professor of public administration at the University of Southern California's Washington Public Affairs Center. He is also president of Wholey Associates, a member of the Virginia Board of Social Services, and president of Hospice of Northern Virginia.

Formerly deputy assistant secretary of Health, Education, and Welfare and director of program evaluation research at the Urban Institute, Professor Wholey has also served on the technical staff of the Institute for Defense Analyses and as assistant professor of mathematics at Rutgers University.

Wholey was an elected official for eight years, serving as member and chairman of the Arlington County Board of Supervisors, and as member and chairman of the Washington Metropolitan Area Transit Authority.

He is a member of the National Academy of Public Administration, and has been recipient of the Evaluation Research Society's Myrdal Prize for Government Service and the American Association for Budget and Program Analysis Distinguished Service Award.

Author of three books — *Federal Evaluation Policy, Zero-Base Budgeting and Program Evaluation,* and *Evaluation: Promise and Performance,* Wholey has also written many articles and papers on evaluation, planning, budgeting, and public management.